The Extraordinary Life of
Bill O'Brien

an Ordinary Arizona Irish Cowboy

Nikos Ligidakis

The Extraordinary Life of
Bill O'Brien

an Ordinary Arizona Irish Cowboy

Nikos Ligidakis

INKWELL PRODUCTIONS®

ISBN: 978-0-9861743-4-6
Library of Congress Control Number: 2015918511

Published by Inkwell Productions
10632 N. Scottsdale Rd, Unit 695
Scottsdale, AZ 85254-5280

Tel. 480-315-3781
E-mail info@inkwellproductions.com
Website www.inkwellproductions.com

Cover by
Michael Woodall
Bob Rink photography

Printed in the United States of America

This book is dedicated to Sarah Sargent Paine O'Brien, Bill's beloved wife of 67 years. She has been the source of strength, stability, determination, and creative inspiration for Bill and for her friends and family.

ACKNOWLEDGMENTS

During the amazing journey of developing his stories, the writer becomes a sponge that observes life and gives it back in the form of ideas. It is a privilege for the writer to flutter in the written words; yet it is a serious responsibility, a responsibility to find hope in any despair, peace in every war, water in the desert and food in every land. However, the most fascinating and rewarding part of this journey is the symbiosis with the characters the writer has created. It is a mysterious and unforgettable union.

This journey is not by any means an easy one. There is that blank page that mocks you, the torment of the elusive words, the martyrdom of a sentence, the unfinished page, and the reconstructed chapter.

It is the time for the writer to plead for help.

It was no different for me from any of the other books that I have written. I needed help. The biggest help came from the person I have the privilege to call my friend, Justin O'Brien. Without his help this book would never have been possible. He walked along with me during this journey, tirelessly doing research, proofreading, and patiently recounting the stories of the incredible life of Bill O'Brien, his Dad. In return I wanted to give him a book about the man his family and friends admired so much.

Justin, I am forever grateful for allowing me to take Bill's journey along with you.

I am also thankful to my friend, fellow writer and author of the "Justice" trilogy, W. Ward Neuman, for helping with the editing of these stories and for constantly encouraging me by telling me that my writing is inspiring.

And, of course, to my companion in life, Helene, for always being willing to help me polish my grammar.

CONTENTS

THIS LAND IS BILL'S LAND 3

THE MEETING 7

THE EARLY YEARS 15

THE GREAT DEPRESSION. 27

YOUNG BILL'S ENTERPRISES 35

BOY SCOUTS AND FLUNKING CATHOLISM 41

BILL'S TRAPLINES AND WILL ROGERS. 45

FISHERMAN BILL AND FARMER'S MARKET 51

COLTURAL DIVERSITY 59

SISTER JANE, The HOLLYWOOD MOVIE STAR 63

ECHOS OF WAR AND MARRIAGE OF JANE AND JUSTIN 67

RUNNING AWAY TO BE A COWBOY 73

PEARL HARBOR AND IWO JIMA. 85

SOUVENIRS AND THE JAPANESE SURRENDER 97

THE PANAMA CANAL 105

THANKSGIVING DAY BOXING MATCH. 109

ARUBA 115

BACK AT UNIVERSITY OF ARIZONA 125

MEETING SADA 129

THE WEDDING AND THE IRISH 135

BILL O'BRIEN WOOL MERCHANT 141

SOUTH AFRICA, ELEPHANTS AND SHARKS 147

PERU, ARGENTINA AND RHODESIAN RIDGEBACKS 157

POLIO AND THE PROMISE 165

MOVE TO ARIZONA 169

PHOENIX IN THE SIXTIES 177

THE PRACTICAL JOKER 185

JACKRABBITS, SNAKES AND MUZZLE LOADER 191

KARTHEEN, LAST HUNT AND THE FIRST SOUTHWEST SBIC 199

ON THE TOP OF THE MOUNTAIN 203

WENDY THE ARTIST, HER STORY 207

CAMELBACK MOUNTAIN: THE HUB OF THE VALLEY AT RISK . . . 215

CITY HALL AUCTION 227

THE MAN AND THE MOUNTAIN 233

EAGLETAIL RANCH 239

BILL O'BRIEN, NATURALIST 245

THE EAGLETAILS 251

CHARLIE RUSSELL, LOVER AND HOME WRECKER 255

THE IMPLICATIONS OF AN IRISH AND SWISS F-1 CROSS 261

BEAUTY CONTEST IN THE PALM GROVE 265

WIND CATCHER, GRASS AND SANDRA DAY O'CONNOR 269

THE HEART OF THE IRISH 273

LOS SAN PATRICIOS 283

THE LONG JOURNEY 289

Author's Bio 301

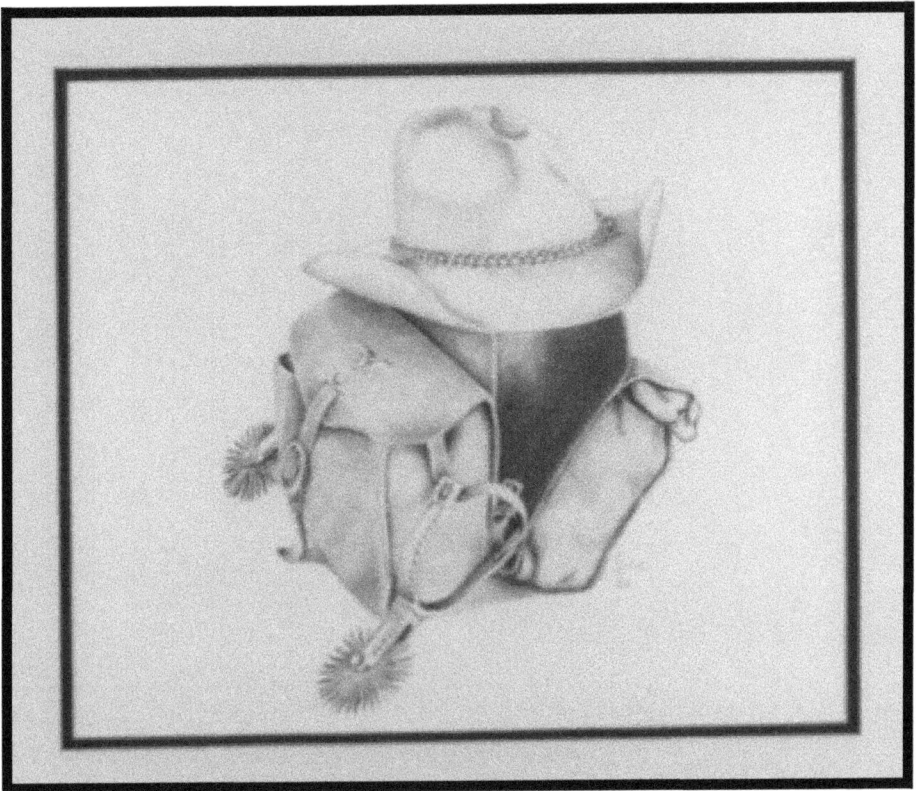

Bill's Gear.

Artist, Wendy Paine O'Brien

THIS LAND IS BILL'S LAND

It was the beginning of the fall, the soil was fragrant, the dewdrops resonating from the citrus trees. A gentle breeze blew and filled my heart with a refreshing dew. Beyond the green paradise there was a treeless land shadowed by mountains.

It was an image of tenderness and strength.

And, there was life, a life that Bill O'Brien had created. I tried to imagine the spirited life that adorned this place just a few decades back. There were sweet grapes hanging from the grapevines and a couple of deer trying to nibble on its fruit. There were jackrabbits running between the alfalfa fields, quail leading their babies, running behind like little fur-balls next to the jojoba sprouts, hundreds of doves cooing on the palm groves and eagles preening in the irrigation ditch, under the peach trees. There were thousands of acres of orchards, including plums and vegetables, mainly cucumbers and pumpkins, unfolded in front of the eyes of my imagination and, beyond that, several people picking cotton. There was an unquestionable ranch lifestyle here with facilities to house workers and to engage in a wide range of activities.

I heard a distant noise from above and looked up on the wide blue sky. I imagined Bill's Cessna-180 airplane flying low above the fields, looking on the graphic view before landing on the five-hundred-foot runway and I felt his joyful look at what he had created.

As the light morning breeze caressed my face I imagined the racetrack beyond the jojoba fields, where the ranchers brought their horses on the weekend for exhilarating races. There were also dog races, not cruel greyhound races but fun, playful dog races. Several dog owners brought their dogs to run around the track and compete.

I heard voices of neighborhood kids taking a safari in the palm grove jungle all the way up to the Elephant's Graveyard and the Leopard's Lair, where Bill had built a heated pool from water that came out of three wells.

Harquahala is an oasis, a green refuge in the midst of the most spectacular desert of Arizona. To the west rose the amazing pinnacles of the Eagletail Mountains, named after a great stone eagle silhouetted against the blue sky. There are deep canyons in this mystifying land and sheer stones walls that guard mysteries unknown even to the local residents. Northeast of the Harquahala ranch is the rugged Saddleback Mountains, popular with rock climbers and a plethora of quality fire agate rocks that brought in weekend prospectors. In between there are ruins of remote Indian villages, petroglyphs on the canyon walls, artifacts from the long past and old gold and silver mines. To the north there are the Big Horn Mountains with the Vulture Peak, a distinctive monolith resting in the far horizon. Herds of desert mules and a few big horn sheep are wandering on the rocky slopes. Just a few miles to the west is the Kofa Mountain, a wildlife refuge and natural habitat, especially for rare mountain sheep. The streets of this community reflect the western lure. They are named after famous cowboys and western artists.

The Harquahala Ranch utilized one well and there are two other wells which were held in reserve. Several water meters have been connected to residences.

People choose to live here because of the fresh air and to get away from the city noise and havoc filled lifestyle.

Bill O'Brien was here, one of a sprinkling of people working in this awe-inspiring western land. It was over twenty thousand acres of unrestrained beauty and an identifiable ecosystem of exceptional natural diversity. The beauty of nature here supports a rare habitat for bighorn sheep, desert tortoise, mule deer herds and a sizable raptor population living among the uncommon cactus formations of chaparral and wild desert grasslands.

High peaks and foothills, deep rocky canyons, valleys, and ridges dropping to gravelly broad slopes from the mountains to a distant landscape.

Harquahala means "running water high up" in the language of one early native tribe, it is named after its numerous perennial creeks and springs. But it is much more than that. The Harquahala Peak is the highest point in southwest Arizona and provides a breathtaking panorama of rugged topography. The area sheltered from canyon's interior drainage system furnishes the solitude and the secluded experience treasured by many wilderness visitors.

From the summit of the peak, the view of the surrounding steep canyons, off-road trails and mountains stretch outwards to hundreds of miles.

There is an obscure trail of over five miles up to the ruins of the remains of an observatory built in the mid-twenties. These impressive places are part of the Outback, an immense piece of land blessed with paramount mountains, surrounded by lost mines and ghost towns. Beneath the mountains spread huge farms and ranches.

This astonishing desert land stretches westward from Phoenix to the Colorado River. It has often been called "The O'Brien's Outback." It was not all Bill O'Brien's outback but he owned and farmed a piece of it, sixteen hundred acres of the Harquahala, and he ran a ranch on seven hundred square miles of public land. Bill is a legend of this big region because he brought life to the desolated real estate and created work for thousands of people. He chose to build an empire in this amazing land and dedicated his days working his ranch and farming fruits and vegetables in this unique and challenging desert soil. He is a part of this land.

I gazed at the Eagletail Ranch that looms above the Harquahala Valley, a spectacular jagged ranch lying across the O'Brien's land. Named after the natural rock structures resembling eagle's plumage, the mountain supports spiny growths of saguaro cacti and below it is a sanctuary for cholla, prickly pears, desert marigold, creosote bushes and blossoms of yellow, purple and red.

Bill O'Brien's philosophy has always been to give back to the land that he takes from and to protect all living things. He has determined that no one will own a piece of the O'Brien's Outback unless they agreed that the land will be a bird and wildlife refuge – forever

THE MEETING

As I drove up the street on the north slope of Camelback Mountain in Paradise Valley, I was infused with a morning serenity that neutralized the tension of the morning commuters. Perched halfway up the mountain was the Elements restaurant at Sanctuary Resort, where my friend Justin O'Brien was waiting for me to discuss his father's biography. We walked to the table where Bill O'Brien was sitting at his favorite spot with a fabulous view of the valley below. He was wearing what I came to learn was Bill O'Brien's cowboy outfit. He had a white custom-made beaver pelt cowboy hat, white long-sleeve cowboy shirt with double front pockets, Western bow tie, red bandana around his neck , pristine dark blue Levis and Charro boots.

Justin and I had been planning this meeting for many weeks. Justin approached the first meeting with his father with me with cautious optimism. He knew I would be in for one of the greatest challenges for any author—how to capture the voice, the spirit, the adventures, and the remarkable character of what seemed to be an unassuming Arizona Irish cowboy. With a boxer's reflexes, Bill stood up with and shook my hand. His handshake was not like one you would expect from a typical ninety-two-year-old man, he had a strong grasp that revealed a lifetime of vigor, athleticism, and a genuine love of people.

His smile was sincere and he looked me right in my eyes, as if to examine my soul.

"You're strong," he said with a youthful smile, "I sure don't want to arm-wrestle you."

I smiled back, trying to apprehend the persona of this man I had heard so much about. We talked for a while, small talk, really. Then he wanted to know all about me. The fact that Bill O'Brien did not talk about himself, but rather was interested in me and my life, revealed a cosmopolitan man who knows how to make someone feel comfortable in his presence. The Elements restaurant staff treated him with the kind of admiration and respect equivalent to a venerable leader. From our table we could see the entire Town of Paradise Valley below. The sun had now become a large orange band, approaching in the east horizon, ready for the long day trip across Arizona's big sky.

Looking at Bill O'Brien, I wondered about this man's lengthy journey and all that he had accomplished. I detected a mysterious smile from him as he observed the landscape below. We were set to start the Bill O'Brien journey, a voyage full of challenge and adventure. His was a story about an ordinary Arizona Irish cowboy, but one with a complex mind who has led an extraordinary life. As he teased out of me details from my own life, I realized what he was doing. He was interviewing me! Just then, Bill looked at me with a disarming smile and said with heartfelt voice, "Nikos, you've had an incredible life. You are such an interesting man," He knew how to praise a person, it was a part of his charming personality, one that had served him well throughout his life. I wanted to tell him that the feeling was mutual, but I decided to wait until I heard the rest of the story.

Before leaving our meeting and, knowing that I spoke Spanish, he said, with a perfect Spanish accent, "Adios amigo. Vaya con Dios."

"Now that we are going to be working together, you have

to learn Greek," I said jokingly.

"Okay, that's next," he said, without batting an eye.

Bill did not say, as you would expect from someone of his age, "I am too old for this." He showed me he was still wide open to learning, in fact he was the epitome of "life-long learning," which was quite an impressive attitude.

As I drove down from The Sanctuary on Camelback Mountain, I was certain I had met an amazing man whose limitless energy, deeply honest smile, and unmistakable strength remained vividly in my mind.

"A cosmopolitan cowboy!" I thought and smiled in amazement.

We met a few days later in the ironically named "The Shedd," a large room in the back of the O'Brien's home. The Shedd is used as a gathering place for celebrations, for power sessions with local business leaders and visiting dignitaries, and as a guest home to top baseball players brought here during Spring Training.

There is nothing flamboyant about this room as it is rather unpretentious.

Bill told me, "We spell The Shedd with two 'd's to keep it noble and dignified."

When you walk into The Shedd, you know you are in a space that reflects Bill O'Brien's world. Western art and books, Irish literature and history, and the interior decoration unmistakably reveals a cowboy's territory. Photographs of Bill with world leaders, famous politicians, captains of industry, and celebrities cover the walls, illustrating the life of a man whose presence has made an enormous difference; a man who seemingly has done just about everything. In two-to three- hour sessions over the next year, The Shedd was to be what Bill called "our stomping grounds," where Bill could tell me his stories, all of which plainly reveal the life of this man whom son Justin affectionately calls, "What You See Is What You Get." And what we see will come to be truly amazing.

Dressed impeccably again in his cowboy attire and beaming his ever-present broad smile, he was ready for our first meeting at the round solid copper-top table.

"Mr. O'Brien, tell me about your years growing up." I asked.

"Well, first of all, call me Bill."

He took a few minutes to reflect the times of long ago. He glanced at Justin who was sitting quietly and spoke only to remind his Dad of something important in the story. It is immediately apparent that Justin highly respects and loves his father—not the usual, "I-respect-my-father" sentiment but one reserved for a great hero, role model, and friend.

"Well, I have so many stories to tell but since we're here with Justin, I'll tell a story about him.

The respect seemed mutual. I looked at Justin, who smiled and shrugged his shoulders, as if to say "Why not?"

"One hot July afternoon, we were driving our old two-door Ford pick-up from Eagletail Ranch to the town of Hyder to buy some cattle when the truck broke down, right in the middle of nowhere."

Bill stopped talking for a moment and signaled Justin to continue the story.

"Yes, I was just ten years old," Justin responded. "I was terrified that we were stuck in 120° degree scorching hot weather in a desert crawling with snakes and turkey vultures flying Lazy 8's over our heads as we baked our last hour together in a broken-down pickup truck. Worst of all, I knew that my father knows less about cars than I do, and, at ten years old, I knew nothing. I thought we were going to die."

Suddenly, Bill jumped out from the pick-up, he popped open the hood, started jiggling a few things and told Justin, "step lively on the gas pedal." Then he stepped back from the hood, tipped up his cowboy hat, rubbed his chin with his leather glove, and remained silent for a few moments. Justin was waiting for him to ask him for a hammer or a screwdriver, or a shovel to dig their graves. The turkey vultures had landed on a nearby Palo Verde tree, and emitted low guttural hissing sounds. To Justin's astonishment, Bill asked, "Justin, take out three sticks of that gum you brought, chew 'em up, and hand the wad over to me on the double."

Justin practically broke the front windshield trying to hand him the gum.

"Is it possible my Dad was an accidental mechanic?" He thought.

Bill bent over the engine and started inserting the freshly chewed gum somewhere. Justin heard wiggling and jiggling and scraping of metal.

"Now hold on." Bill said. "Now wait. Now watch. Now turn the key."

The engine roared to life as Justin stepped on the gas. The buzzards flew away their hearts broken, and Justin's heartbeat resumed normal behavior.

"How could you possibly fix our truck out here in the desert?" Justin asked his Dad.

"Justin, when you don't know what you're doing, the trick is to act like you know what you're doing." Bill replied.

As we sat in The Shedd, Bill took a deep cleansing breath, obviously proud how his son had recounted so vividly the story of Bill's mechanical dexterity in the desert, a story that happened fifty years earlier. I could sense his mind rewinding our conversation, like a fly fisherman, back to my previous question. I realized that this was going to be a lengthy journey. I was ready for the ride.

"I was born and grew up in the Los Angeles area...," he said. And for the next three hours, Bill captivated me with stories about his tough, but loving Irish family, his adolescent and teenage years, his Army Cavalry and his U.S. Navy career, meeting his wife, Sada, his business deals, farming, being an inventor, a boxer, an activist and so much more. He mesmerized my mind into his world of mystery, intrigue, adventure and above all character.

Bill told his stories with apparent fascination, as if the life he was talking about wasn't his, but as if it was the life he wanted to live. It was when he spoke about running away from home to be a cowboy that I noticed that his cowboy accent grew thicker in the memories of different times and places. Even though Bill O'Brien was now ninety-two-years-old and his memory was slowly fading, he was sharp and witty. At 5'6", he was not a big man. But when you talked with him, you felt his presence; he commanded the space around him, while giving others plenty of room to breathe. And even on one of our last days of interviews, Bill O'Brien told me he did sixty stomach crunches and lifted twenty-pound weights, all while calling out multiplication tables. Implausible? Yes. Hard to believe? For certain. But his son Justin tells me he has seen his Dad in doing his exercise routine.

Over the next year, as we grew to know each other, I discovered Bill O'Brien was also a: storyteller, entrepreneur, naturalist, poet, philanthropist, rancher, farmer, pilot, sailor, falconer, polo player, boxer, wool merchant, archer, jockey, dog breeder, globetrotter, practical joker, alligator roper, bronc rider and so much more. With his snow-white hair, broad smile, and steel-grey eyes that still twinkled with amusement when he was excited about something, Bill O'Brien never lost the sparkle of life. At no point did I ever hear him speak ill of anyone, and he never complained about past adversities. He had a way to appreciate everyone with whom he came in contact.

Enough stories for the first day, enough. For me it was time to go, as my head was spinning as I tried to absorb all I had heard. I knew that it was going to be a challenge to capture this man's persona, his voice and his spirit all on paper, but I was up for the challenge. Before leaving The Shedd, Bill gathered several write-ups and books related to his life story and handed them to me. He acted as if he wanted to help with my research but I sensed that this incredible man already trusted me with his life story, and we had already become good friends. One of the items he handed to me was "The Patrick Murray Clan" a book about his family's roots on his mother's side. He autographed it and wrote in Spanish, "To El Griego, el Rey de Los Griegos."

Yes, Mr. O'Brien, right back at you with the respect. We walked back down to the house. Their large female Rhodesian Ridgeback dog greeted the three of us, wagging her tail and whacking out melodies with it as she brushed against the cast iron posts on the kitchen wood block cutting table. The aroma of homemade cookies enticed my nostrils. The television was playing a movie with Fred Astaire dancing with Ginger Rogers. Bill's wife, Sada, turned around and smiled as Bill walked towards her. He bent down to kiss her, "I love you Sada." "I love you too," She responded, reaching for his hand.

"They've been saying that every day for the last sixty-seven years," Justin quietly said.

THE EARLY YEARS

Bill's father, James Matthew O'Brien, grew up as an Irish-American orphan in Chicago during the late 1800's. As a child, he was shuttled from one distant Irish relative to another relative that he hardly knew. Eventually, the welcome mat from the relatives wore out, and he spent most of his childhood bouncing from orphanage to orphanage. James realized that his only way out from that miserable life was education. As he grew, he began to read every good book available to him. In the early days of the 1900's, teenager James was determined to make something out of his life.

Since the turn of the nineteenth century, Chicago had been a popular city for immigrants. Its population growth is credited to private free enterprise. A bewildering number of privately held companies had began moving to Chicago. The population growth played an enormous role in the expansion of the elevated railroad system and other important infrastructural projects. Thousands of jobs were created as Chicago built out its early urban transportation systems to accommodate the city's rapid development.

James O'Brien, now a grown man with a tremendous amount of determination and an adventurous spirit, knew that Chicago was the city where he could make his mark and surpass the miseries of his unfortunate early youth. He discovered if he could pass the entrance exam to law school, it counted more than the academic background. Because of his great love for learning by reading, he passed the entrance exam at the Washington and Lee School of Law in Virginia. He was planning to work hard to pay for his education, but one of his father's cousins offered to pay for James' education.

The unexpected fortune allowed James to focus on becoming a lawyer. After a great deal of study and hard work, he was able to get his law degree. His dream was always to go back to Chicago but his college roommate and best friend, Hi Dow, convinced James to find his fortune in New Mexico. Hi's father was a partner in a successful law firm in Roswell, New Mexico. After graduation, James and Hi traveled to Roswell and joined the law firm, Hervey, Hinkle and Dow as clerks. James was an ambitious young man and at age twenty-two, he was elected county attorney of Eddy County, New Mexico.

That was where James met Irene Murray, a beautiful red-haired Irish young girl, and they fell in love. Irene Murray was born in Fort Sill, Oklahoma. She called herself an "Army brat," as her family always moved to where her military father was transferred. Her father, Michael Steven Murray, was from Ireland and entered United States through Canada. Michael Murray joined the Army and rose up to the rank of Captain. In those days, it was quite rare for an Irishman to get promoted to such a high rank.

Captain Michael Murray moved west under General Pershing's command to help maintain peace with the Indians. He and his family were transferred to Roswell, New Mexico, where he taught U.S. History, music, mathematics, and polo at the New Mexico Military Institute.

James O'Brien, who was then twenty-four years old, finished his term as county attorney of Eddy County, New Mexico. He decided to move to Los Angeles because he saw it was the land of opportunity. Later, Captain Murray and his family were transferred to The Old Soldiers' Home in Los Angeles on Wilshire and Sawtelle, where he served his remaining military years as Quartermaster.

James and Irene, were married and honeymooned in the Redwood Forest north of San Francisco. They had a girl and three boys—Jane, Jim, Bill, and Don— a third generation Irish-American kids.

William Howard O'Brien was born in the Hollywood Hospital on Sunset Boulevard on February 25, 1923, in the middle of what historians now call, The Roaring Twenties. It was a time of American prosperity and cultural influence. World War I had ended in 1918, jazz music was all the rage, and consumer demand for modern American-made products was on the rise. The fervent patriotism for American soldiers during the war seemed to transfer over to an extravagant focus on sports athletes and movie stars.

Bill was the third child of James and Irene Murray O'Brien. One of the most challenging tasks for the new O'Brien parents in the early days was to deal with the terrible raging temper of Baby Bill, especially when his milk bottle was taken away from him before he was through. Red faced and husky-lunged, Baby Bill demanded his bottle. In his desperate baby tantrums, he screamed for his bottle even though he couldn't pronounce the words. His words that screeched out were, "Boboo! Boboo!" The word stuck, so "Boboo" is what he and the entire O'Brien family and friends called Bill's mother. James O'Brien was given his own nickname by the four children, "Poppy."

So the O'Brien parents were always known to family and friends as "Boboo and Poppy." Everyone who knew them said they were the perfect couple. They stayed deeply in love for the rest of their lives, regardless of circumstances. They ran a strict house, but their love for their four children was obvious to everyone who knew them. Between Irene's Catholic discipline and common-sense practicality, blended with James' love of learning, strong ambition, and precise speaking and writing skills, the three O'Brien boys and one girl had the best of all possible worlds growing up.

Irene O'Brien usually only had to tell the four children one time to do something. If they didn't, their Mother would give them The Look. If that parenting tactic didn't work, Irene O'Brien would physically give them her fearsome, Pressure on the Arm, a mostly harmless but instantly understood gesture that underscored her Irish determination that Mother should be obeyed or else. Years later, Bill would use that parenting technique on his own children. Because of his strength and his temper, Bill would never spank his children. Instead, he would lay them over his knee and calmly talk to them about the consequences of their actions. Although he spared the rod, he educated his children as to the errors of their ways, and they loved him for it.

James O'Brien taught the O'Brien kids that education and learning was the key to success and happiness, whether you learn in college or on the job. Poppy loved Mark Twain's expression, "I have never let my schooling interfere with my education." He also taught the young O'Briens the power of words, excellent grammar, and precise speech. In the 1930s, the expression, "Cool!" had not caught on yet, but everyone used to say "Swell!" The O'Brien children would never even say "Swell!" around Poppy, because they knew he wouldn't let them butcher the English language in front of him. So Bill, Don, Jim, and Jane developed their own coded kids' words.

One of Poppy's gifts was storytelling, a talent Bill O'Brien would develop and perfect his whole life. Poppy told the kids about his life in The Territory of New Mexico before it became a state. He regaled them with stories of real cowboys, actual Indians living on the plains, the Texas Rangers, and sagas of the Old West. Some stories Poppy had first-or second-hand knowledge. For example, he told of the outlaw, Billy the Kid, and Pat Garrett, the sheriff of Lincoln County, who caught and killed Billy the Kid. One of the partners of Poppy's first law firm, Hervey, Hinkle and Dow was James Hervey. While Attorney General of the Territory of New Mexico, James Hervey had been directly involved in investigating the murder of Pat Garrett. Fifteen years before television took over the American living room, Poppy O'Brien kept the four kids riveted and spell-bound as they listened in amazement to their father's stories.

Poppy Jim also knew Indian sign language. One of the most memorable stories was about his sister, Josephine. She was kidnapped by the Indians at the age of twelve and for two weeks was held captive by the Indians in Oklahoma Territory. James' uncle tracked them down on horseback and got her back.

The Roaring Twenties were booming years in Los Angeles. It was the time when Bill's father, James O'Brien, had a successful law firm specializing in real estate and water rights law, and his investments flourished. This was the period of American history known as Prohibition, and alcohol had been declared illegal. The increase of the illegal production and sale of liquor known as bootlegging led to the proliferation of illegal drinking spots known as speakeasies. The related rise in gang violence and other crimes led to decreased support for Prohibition by the end of the 1920s. Consequently, the entire country was on a threshold of economic expansion.

The O'Brien's had built a beautiful Southern-style mansion on South Rossmore Street in Hancock Park.

Bill's mother and father played tennis with friends at the Rossmore house every Sunday after church. Young Bill was four years old and he thought watching tennis was almost as boring as church. He spent much of his time with Mattie Staples, a wonderful African-American lady who worked in the O'Brien's house as their nanny. It was a hot, sunny day when Mattie and Bill were walking around the lawn in front of the house. "Who are you talking to, Billy O'Brien?" Mattie looked at the kid with her big dark eyes as she heard him talking to himself.

"I am talking to my friend, Kartheen, "Bill answered without blinking an eye.

"Who is Kartheen and where is he, child?" Mattie played along.

"He's sitting on my shoulder," Bill responded with an innocent voice, pointing on his right shoulder

"Can he hear me? If so, say hello from me." Mattie said smiling.

Mattie had to go inside the house to finish her chores

She told him, "Stay close to the house. Don't be wandering around the neighborhood."

She knew Bill well. Yet, young Bill, now all alone, suddenly stripped off all his clothes and streaked across the one-acre lawn, naked as a jaybird, and hid under a row of bushes. When he saw Mattie coming out of the house he crept along the other side of the bushes, across the yard and climbed a tall weeping willow tree. He didn't think Mattie would see him because, according to Kartheen, his imaginary pal, hardly anybody looks up. Well, eventually she did look up but not after about an hour and a half. It was one of the few times Bill saw Mattie angry.

"You come down from that tree right now!" Mattie had a reason to be concerned since kidnapping was pretty common in those days. "Who gave you such an idea as to run away like that?"

"It was Kartheen's idea. He told me I was safe up in the tree," Bill yelled from the top of the tree.

"Well, you tell Kartheen that I want both of you down out of that tree right now."

Her voice reverberated across the serene neighborhood. When Mattie was mad you had to obey. Kartheen and Bill climbed out of the tree together

"And tell your friend to obey me, you hear?" she said as they were walking back to the house.

"Kartheen says hello back to you. I wish you could see him,'" Bill responded.

"I can't see him because he sits on top of your shoulder, but I can hear you two talking sometimes."

Bill held Mattie's hand, looked up and smiled, thinking about how secure and loved he felt around her. Bill never talked about Kartheen around his sister or brothers because they would say he was crazy, but Mattie accepted them both.

For Bill and his brothers and sisters, growing up in the twenties in Los Angeles were happy days. Bill loved his big sister Jane, older brother Jim, and his younger brother, Don. Jane was always doing grown-up things like taking dancing lessons and playing tennis with her friends or going swimming at someone's house. Jim, Bill, and Don rambled all over town like the little gang of Irish-American kids that they were. James O'Brien's law practice and real estate investments brought prosperity to the O'Brien household.

In the summer of 1929, the O'Brien family piled into their seven-passenger Buick to vacation in their second home in Clear Lake, north of the wine country and east of Mt. St. Helena. Clear Lake, was a natural freshwater lake fed by runoff flowing into many streams. Abundant fish, game, and waterfowl made Clear Lake an oasis in the mountainous

Lake County, which later became part of the breathtaking California's wine region country. It was a long winding drive in that big Buick, especially for the kids, but it was worth the trip. These were working vacations for Poppy Jim, who was always a sharp investor and businessman. He owned a great deal of real estate up there, including the water company, and he was developing a property. Poppy understood cash flow and how to keep costs down.

"Profit is like food," he would advise young Bill, who wanted to know what Poppy knew about making money, "but cash flow is like water. And, without water, in a few days, you're all dried up."

Boboo always carried a small tree branch with a few leaves left on the tip, and used it without warning as a switch whenever the kids were fighting in the back seat. She rarely had to use it, but the four kids could see it in plain view in the front seat. The switch didn't hurt much but that it sure kept the kids quiet for a while. There were many stops along the way. One of them was halfway where they stopped at the beautiful Pismo Beach to eat clams. They always stopped at the neighborhood of Saugus in Santa Clarita to drink buttermilk before going over the winding road of Mt. Saint Helena. Those curves were too much for the kids sitting and swaying in the back seat, and sometimes they had to stop and upchuck. Boboo knew the buttermilk could settle their queasy stomachs and it usually worked. They also stopped at a Franciscan monastery in the wine country. Poppy would go inside while Boboo and the four kids would wait in the Buick. Ten minutes later, Poppy Jim would come out with the Abbot of the Franciscan monastery, followed by two monks in traditional brown robes with their white belts. The abbot gave some kind of blessing the kids couldn't hear, then he made the sign of the cross. Bill notice the abbot held his fingers in a peculiar way and asked his brother Jim what that meant.

"The Father makes his fingers in a way that actually spells out the letters IC XC, which means Jesus Christ," said brother Jim, jabbing Bill sharply in the ribs. "You're supposed to know this, Bill. You'll have to go to Catholic confirmation in a few years. I doubt you'll pass and become a Catholic."

On the drive up, the family had to stop at a shoe store because his son Jim said he had a big hole in his high top Keds sneakers. Keds sneakers, so called because you could sneak around in them, were a big hit with American kids. Son Jim picked out a brand new pair, identical to his beige Keds. Poppy gave Jim the two dollars to pay the shoe clerk; he wanted his son to feel like a grown up by paying. They headed back to the car. Poppy, thinking about his Clear Lake businesses, not seem very happy spending the two dollars, and that sure didn't help his attitude.

"Take good care of these shoes," Poppy said to his son, putting his hand on Jim's shoulder.

As they drove the winding road over Mt. Saint Helena, all four kids started to get car sick. Boboo, always thinking ahead, brought out from an ice chest four bottles of buttermilk and told them to drink it. All his life Bill loved his buttermilk.

During that trip, Jim put on the right shoe of the Keds sneakers. He rolled down the window, told his brothers and sisters to watch, and hurled what he thought was the old right sneaker out the Buick car window. They watched the sneaker bounce down the mountain ravine until it was out of side.

He then put on the left Keds sneaker and again threw the other left Keds out the window.

A few minutes later, a mortified Jim, looking down at his feet, shouted to Poppy that he accidentally threw out both the new Keds sneakers by mistake. The children never saw their dad so mad before. Poppy made a quick U-turn with the Buick station wagon and sped back to the scene of the crime, some five miles down the winding mountain road. Jim, Bill, and Don barreled out of the car while Jane looked on, and the boys clambered down the ravine swiftly to retrieve Jim's shoes. Jim found the first one. Bill ran down the ravine and found the other new sneaker, and ran back, shouting to his brothers, and held up the precious new Keds shoe triumphantly with his right arm. The three boys clawed their way up the ravine, scrambled into the Buick, and they drove off. Nobody spoke for a while, then Bill, struggling to suppress a laugh, couldn't hold it any longer. He smiled at Jim, and Jim started to chuckle, which made Don and Jane burst out laughing. Then, Poppy and Boboo looked back at their four kids, and they all burst out laughing.

Bill's sister, Jane, was a popular girl at Clear Lake. She rode horses, dove off the high tower into the lake, and once swam three miles across the lake to the other side. Bill couldn't imagine himself swimming that far, but he finally got the nerve to jump off the high tower. He made friends with two local boys, Gordon and Bob. One of their exciting ideas was to make wooden spears out of tree branches to go skunk hunting. That idea turned into a disaster when they came home all smelling like skunk. They also put on a rodeo show called "O'Brien's Buckaroos" and made a grand total of seventy-eight cents. Those summers were exhilarating and, of course, they dreaded the time they had to go back to school.

Bill liked to fight, or rather, he enjoyed fighting to gain respect on account of his small stature. Many of the bigger kids picked on him mercilessly, which toughened his soul and his hide. One day he was fighting a kid who was slightly bigger than him. Bill's imaginary friend, Kartheen, was telling him to "Give it all you've got!" Unfortunately, all Bill had was not good enough to subdue his larger opponent. Another kid decided to be the peacemaker and stepped up to save Bill from the embarrassment of defeat. His name was Sanford Rosenbaum and they became friends for life. Bill never forgot that Sanford saved him from being whipped and shamed.

THE GREAT DEPRESSION

Everything seemed to be moving along, until the Great Depression hit the country and America spun out of control into an economic downturn. On October 29, 1929, the stock market crashed and wiped out the savings of millions of investors. Soon after the Depression began, consumer spending and investments dropped, causing steep declines in industrial output and rising levels of unemployment. Failing companies laid off workers by the tens of thousands and eventually millions of Americans were unemployed. Half of the country's banks shut their doors.

Poppy Jim was one of the millions who lost most of his money during the Depression. It was a time of survival and scarcity. The Roaring Twenties were muzzled, and luxuries and frivolous spending were no longer possible. America's Great Depression was getting worse for James O'Brien. Eventually he lost the mansion at South Rossmore and had to move in to a place called "Brentwood." Boboo had found a seven-room house for sale on top of a hill at 254 Tigertail Road that had been owned by someone else who also went broke.

To the O'Brien family's great disappointment, they had to let go of Mattie and Spence, her husband, the chauffeur. They traded in the seven-passenger Buick for a Model B Ford. As with millions of distraught Americans, the O'Brien family had to make agonizing readjustments. But for Bill, it was like breaking into a new life of freedom. He felt that life for him was going to be great in the country around Brentwood Hills. He felt sorry for his parents because he saw the quiet desperation on their faces. They had lost everything in the Depression, yet they remained stoic and resolved to overcome their enormous economic setbacks. Their strength and determination to climb back up the ladder of prosperity was forever instilled in his psyche, and he started to conceive of endless ways to make money and support the family. Thus, the seeds of optimism and can-do spirit were planted in young Bill O'Brien.

The four kids were born about five years apart, so Boboo had her hands full. Jane went to Marymont, a Catholic girl's school in the hills behind Westwood. Jim started at University High in Sawtelle, and Don and Bill went to Brentwood Grammar School. Patriotism was big even in grammar school. All children had to stand still and salute the American flag as it was raised and recite the Pledge of Allegiance every day before class.

The move to the new house on top of the hill brought the family closer together, as they were living in a smaller house and without household help. Boboo did the cooking, Jane set the table and the three boys did the dishes and many other household chores. There was a spectacular view from the hill, with greenery extending as far as the eye could see and to the endless ocean. Entering Brentwood Grammar School was kind of scary at first for young Bill. Boboo dropped him off for the first day in school. Bill acted tough, like a cowboy, pretending that he wasn't scared.

"Well, so long, Boboo," he told his mother stoically as she drove away. He stood puzzled as to what to do next until a lady teacher steered him with her hands into a classroom.

Los Angeles, the "City of Angels" was a fast-growing metropolis. Silent movies were in and so was radio. Cowboy silent movie star Tom Mix was popular, but he couldn't make the transition when sound movies came in. They said the cowboy's voice was too squeaky and high.

The road from the top of the hill, where the O'Brien family now lived, curved down like a tiger's tail to Sunset Boulevard. This shape gave it the name "Tigertail Road." The family seemed to be adjusting well, and, in fact, grew to love this new location. Brentwood was not considered to be a swinging town but it was beautiful. Bill's father often said, "This place will someday be a popular destination." And it did become just that. Today it is a community of expensive homes where many celebrities live.

For the children, to grow up in this new environment without a nanny to control them, gave them the opportunity to explore new and fascinating things. There were other kids in the neighborhood and pretty soon they made new, inseparable friends. Bill and his friends created their own entertainment. Once they made a wagon out of old planks and wagon wheels found in the dump and hurtled down Tigertail Road. The only way they could slow down was to wedge an old broomstick handle under the axle of the coaster on the asphalt road. It was a dangerous game, but at that age, kids are immune to the thought of danger. They just wanted to feel the excitement of the unknown, of adventure. They held big races down the hill where many wagons entered. The races were about a mile downhill and often the momentum would build up until it was too late to slow down, and their broomstick handles smoldered into a blaze of fire. Many times they would crash and their wagons would be obliterated. The kids would return home with scratched knees and elbows, happier, and wiser.

Bill's close friend was Bub Eschrich, a Swiss kid who lived across the street from the O'Briens. They made a toboggan out of an old tin real estate sign and they would slide down on the slippery wild oats. After two or three trips, the bottom of the sign got shiny, the grass got slippery and the slide got longer and much faster. That makeshift toboggan built up quite a bit of speed going down that hill, and it stimulated their thirst for flight. So the two boys decided to build a giant glider out of bamboo and bed sheet that would carry one pilot. They had been building balsam gliders from kits that actually would glide. Bill found most of the parts and Bub did most of the building of their glider. Bill, being lighter, was going to be the pilot. They would use the same broad knoll where they raced their tin sign toboggan. There were plenty of wild oats that cushion a possible crash landing. And there was always a good breeze from the ocean for good lift.

Kid inventor Bub finally finished the glider. It was made of light bamboo that was curved to hold the sheets tight and had an eighteen-foot wing span with a braced hole in the middle for the pilot. Bill's arms were strapped to the braces so his body wouldn't slip through the hole if he got too high in the air. Their moment in glory had arrived. Bill started running down the hill into the oncoming ocean breeze. By golly, it worked! He was three feet off the ground; he was actually flying over the wild oats in the field. Then disaster struck. An exhilarated young Bill suddenly looked down to see how high he was flying. His shifting movement tilted the wing downward, and he flipped completely over and slammed his butt hard on the ground. His arms felt like they were pulled out of their sockets and his head was spinning.

"It's not like you see in the funny papers." Bill said to me, interrupting his reverie in The Shedd to clarify, "You don't see tweeting birdies. It's more like spheres spinning over your head."

The glider was ruined, so they just tossed it in the dump on the way home. Bub wanted to build a bigger better glider, but Bill told him it was his turn to be the pilot. He never did build it. Despite the failed attempt, the excitement of flying was forever instilled in Bill's heart. And he learned to always look up, not down or back.

There were other interesting games the kids played, like marbles. Bill was pretty good at the game. He had a pouch of marbles, including "Doughboys," "Steelies," and "Aggies" that he got in a trade. Aggies were marbles made of agate that were heavier than regular marbles. They could knock a regular marble out of the ring pretty easily.

Bill was very competitive and learned the business of trading and bartering at a young age. He also recognized and appreciated the ability of a worthy opponent, a talent valuable for any competition. For example, when they flew kites in a competition with the Chinese and Mexican kids, they all used old straight edge razors and the tops of tin cans tied to the arms of the kite. The game was to slash the other kites or to cut another kid's string to bring it down. It was great fun and Bill recognized that the Japanese kids had the best kites and were far superior at flying a kite.

Young Bill began to realize that being Irish had a little stigma to it. Many times he heard some people reacting to his parents after hearing the name "O'Brien."

"Oh, Irish, eh?" they would snort with a voice of contempt.

The kids were told to answer, "Yeah, and proud of it."

"Don't ever back down," was the advice from their parents. The three brothers, Bill, Jim, and Don, had to take boxing lessons every Wednesday night from old Mexican former professional boxers. It cost twenty-five cents for two hours and they were taught how to cock their shoulder into a right jab and lift up the right heel just before the strike. That gave the jab more power and more leveraged weight than they have. The training developed their character. All arguments between brothers were settled with the gloves on, especially when Dad was not home.

The brothers Don and Bill still had to go to boxing lessons until Bill got braces on his teeth. He didn't get into many fights, but with those braces on he didn't want to anyway. The braces were hateful. It made Bill wonder, "Was I beginning to stay out of fights to protect my teeth, or did kids not want to fight anyone with braces?"

After the Japanese farmers harvested their Lima bean fields, Boboo would tell her three sons to go down the hill and glean the dried beans that the harvester missed. She told them that it was okay, "Just don't tell your father," they were warned by Boboo.

She didn't want Poppy to feel worse than he already did for not making money like he used to. Bill learned the importance of maintaining one's dignity and saving face during hard times.

In 1932, the "Tarzan The Ape Man," was a spectacular box office hit. It starred Johnny Weissmuller, an Olympic swimming athlete who won five Olympic gold medals, and numerous other national and world swimming awards. He was a true American role model and every boy, including Bill and his brothers Jim and Don, wanted to be like him. In backyards and playgrounds all across the country, kids would shout the now familiar yodeling Tarzan yell.

Movie director William Van Dyke had Sunday neighborhood pool parties in his home at the bottom of Tigertail Road near the O'Brien family. All kinds of Hollywood movie stars showed up at those parties, but Bill could only recognize those who were in Tarzan or cowboy movies. One Sunday Bill showed up at the party and could not believe his eyes when he saw Tarzan swimming in the director's pool. Since Bill always had his swimming trunks on under his pants, he jumped in. Johnny Weissmuller swam the length of the pool and Bill went after him trying to keep up.

Johnny looked back, smiled and said, "Come on, boy, you can do better than that."

"Mr. Weissmuller, you're too fast. I don't think anyone could catch you." Bill responded.

"All right then, you did great. Let me give you a ride," Tarzan said with a wide smile. "Climb on my back."

Tarzan swam so fast the waves splashed over his back into Bill's face. He could barely hang on as they plowed through the water. Bill said it was the best ride ever.

Another time, the teenage actor Mickey Rooney came with a miniature electric boat that looked like the Queen Mary. Bill was curious to see it run, "Let's put it in and see if it works."

"Nah, I don't want to," Rooney replied. He was bothered by the kid asking questions.

"Why did you bring it if you didn't want to put it in the water?" Bill insisted.

"Listen, kid, I decided not to," Rooney replied grumpily and walked off with his boat.

Bill thought Mickey Rooney was kind of weird because the boy actor brought a fancy boat but he didn't want to actually have fun playing with it. What's the fun in that? Bill though he could take him in a fight because he was about his size. Bill thought that being in the center of attention was a good way to make people dislike you. He realized it was more important to be interested in other people than it was to make them think you are interesting.

The family had a cocker spaniel mix named Val. She had seven puppies, by mistake, so far as Bill could tell. After six weeks, Val quit feeding them.

One Sunday, after Mass, Mother said, "Take those puppies down on Sunset Boulevard and sell them all today, and I mean it."

When Mother said, "I mean it." the kids new they had better listen. So Bill and his brother Don made some signs out of cardboard that read "Puppies: 25 Cents." They put the seven puppies in their wagon and hiked down to Sunset with Val on a length of clothesline rope. Bill placed signs staked out on Sunset Boulevard at a distance far enough to give people driving time to stop. Don was positioned a hundred yards up the road, and he waived a sign to signal the cars to pull over. When the cars stopped, Bill showed them the fine mother of the pups, and the seven puppies sold fast. The boys were happy to report to Mother that they were all sold and she was glad that she didn't have to buy any more canned dog food for those pups. From that experience, Bill learned you have to give buyers a moment to know what you are selling, plus show some credibility as he did with the healthy, well-mannered mother of the pups.

YOUNG BILL'S ENTERPRISES

Times were still tough in the early 1930s. All the excesses of the 1920's was blamed on Hoover when he became president in 1929, only seven months before the Great Depression. Hoover had been a geologist and made a fortune in mining operations overseas. President Hoover started the construction of Hoover Dam but was voted out of office four years later in the middle of the Great Depression. Hoover's approach to the country's economic challenges was to let the economy work itself out.

"Tough it out - no handouts," Hoover would say. He was defeated by Roosevelt in 1932 by a landslide.

After several years living on Tigertail Road, it was time to move on due to financial reasons. Mother found a buyer for the Tigertail Road house for more than it cost, and the family moved to a less expensive house on Bristol Drive across from Brentwood Country Club. The O'Brien children had mixed feelings. They were glad that the sale of the house made some money, but they hated to leave the old neighborhood and friends behind. Mother told the children that Father did all the negotiating on the transaction because he was so smart. But Bill's imaginary friend, Kartheen, told Bill it was really her idea. Whomever was responsible, they all were thankful because the children got new shoes and new clothes. Mother and Father never ever talked in front of the children about money, "except when Mother would tell me to go out and earn some," Bill will often say.

The Brentwood Golf Course, across the street, was a fascinating place. It was always neat and trimmed and well-watered to keep the lush green grass intact. To save money, Father dropped out of the exclusive Los Angeles Country Club on Wilshire Boulevard and joined the Brentwood Country Club, which had a public golf course across the street. According to Father, in the 1930s "The Los Angeles Country Club did not allow Blacks, Jews or movie actors, and they barely tolerated the Irish."

Bill found a spot where the golfers would hit the ball on a great circle swing out into the street. He would go and pick them up, bring them back and sometimes earn a nickel or a dime. That experience taught him you have to keep a sharp eye out for opportunity and always move fast, because that opportunity can disappear in an instant.

Bill was always in need of money so he could help support his family, but also because the more money he made, the more he could buy things he liked. Since it was obvious no one, especially President Hoover, was going to give him any handouts, he decided to answer an ad on the school bulletin board to sell Saturday Evening Posts, a nationally circulated general interest magazine. His job was to go around the neighborhood, knock on doors, and sell magazine subscriptions. For every five-cent Post he sold each week, he would get to keep two cents. He built up a delivery route of sixty customers which netted about one dollar and twenty cents a week. He would have sold more but pushing his bike up the mile-long Tigertail Road to new customers would take too much time after school. After a couple of years he sold his route for a significant amount of cash, plus he went around with the new owner and introduced him to Bill's former customers. "Word of mouth referrals are key. And any time spent away from face to face with a customer is a waste of time," Bill would later advise his son Justin.

After that, he started an at-home car wash business on Saturdays. Following the same rules of success from his Saturday Evening Post magazine route, he built it up, he sold it to another kid for cash. Bill knew the importance of having an exit strategy, no matter how good the business.

One afternoon, Don and Bill were upstairs bouncing a rubber ball in the hallway, when suddenly the ball seemed to start moving sideways in mid-air. Val, their crossbred dog, began barking furiously, and they thought it was some man trying to get in to the house   "What's going on?" Bill looked at his brother.

"That's not the ball, it's the whole house," Don yelled.

They both screamed, "Earthquake," and dashed to their emergency exit, the outside staircase. The whole house shook but, other than some broken dishes, nothing was ruined. The earthquake only lasted a couple of minutes but everybody talked about it for months. Years later, Bill learned that he and Don had lived through a magnitude 6.3 earthquake on March 10, 1933. One hundred and twenty people lost their lives, and Los Angeles suffered millions in property damage. That earthquake was so severe that California changed the building codes to make buildings more earthquake-proof. From that experience, Bill always made sure the homes he bought were structurally sound, even in earthquake-free Arizona because, you never know until it's too late.

Cowboys were in, so Bill formed a gang and decided to call themselves "The California Chapter of the Texas Rangers." The boys already had camping gear, so the Texas Rangers camped out a lot. Since they all had bikes, they could go a lot further from home. A can of vegetable soup, a hot dog and an orange is all you needed for an overnight.

Camping made Bill very self-sufficient, which helped him later as a cowboy. They made Bill's dad a Texas Ranger and swore him in. After that Bill was the only kid in his family that could call his father Jim since Bill was the Camp Captain. Bill's Texas Rangers were still going strong with up to eleven members. They met or hiked about twice a month. Bill's father knew an artist in Roswell, New Mexico so he asked him to help make a logo for the club. The artist painted a smoking Colt 45, a saddle and some spurs and wrote the charter words in fancy lettering. All Texas Ranger members signed in their own blood, which took about three hours of procrastinating on how to draw blood without pain. With some help from Father, they sent the beautifully engraved charter to Governor Allred of Texas, who signed it and put the Great Seal of Texas on it. To this day, the "Great Charter of the California Chapter of the Texas Rangers." hangs in The Shedd at Bill's home. This experience taught Bill to always go to the top if you know what you want and always see them face to face. Years later, the successive mayors of the City of Phoenix would get used to seeing Bill O'Brien, dressed in his finest cowboy attire, cooling his cowboy boot heels in the lobby, with no appointment, just to ask the mayor a quick question.

After a year, it was getting harder to gather the Texas Rangers together for meetings. Most of the boys had to work on Saturdays and after school. Later that year, in 1933, Harry Jennings, the father of two of the Rangers, Harry Jr. and David, had co-invented with Herbert Everest a folding wheel chair made out of lightweight, collapsible steel and bicycle wheels. Called the Everest and Jennings Wheel Chairs, the company manufactured the first wheelchair that could be put in the trunk of a car. Harry's two sons had to help assemble wheelchairs in the Jennings' garage. In 1933, President Roosevelt bought one of the wheelchairs. Business really picked up after that and the company expanded out of the garage to a small factory plant on La Brea Blvd. From that, Bill learned the value a celebrity could bring almost overnight to a business.

California Chapter of The Texas Rangers.

BOY SCOUTS AND FLUNKING CATHOLISM

It was time to join the Boy Scouts. With his energy, enthusiasm, and keen intelligence, Bill naturally gravitated toward leadership roles, so he became first patrol leader.

The members of the patrol met in their hideout. To get there, they would have to climb a tree to make it on the roof of the Janz Investment Real Estate office on the corner of San Vicente and Bundy in Los Angeles. Bill would bring one of his mother's cigarettes from home when his patrol would meet early before Scout meetings. He would light it and pass it around so everyone could take a puff, including his brother, Don, who was the youngest. The cigarette tasted awful but Bill said that cowboys in the movies all smoked and it seemed the manly thing to do. They all swore to keep it quiet because otherwise Bill would be the one to get the razor strap, and he sure didn't want that again. Kids smoking was taboo, but that's why they did it. It sure helped the attendance of his patrol. He learned sometimes you have to take a little risk to get ahead.

Father had a small stock interest in a tuna cannery called Chicken of the Sea. The company was having tough times and paid dividends to stockholders in canned tuna. The O'Brien family ate a lot of tuna during the Depression. Father once arranged for a Japanese fishing boat to take the Texas Rangers to Catalina Island, provided they could raise the money to pay the captain. The boys scoured the neighborhood gathering coat hangers to sell. They also went to any new houses that were being built and gathered empty milk bottles left by the workers. It was easy to sell the bottles to the market and coat hangers to the laundry. They pooled all their money to pay the captain of a Japanese fishing boat called the "Maroo." What a trip! The boys went to the isthmus on the far side of Catalina Island. They dove off the boat and swam ashore, carved pipes out of soapstone and tried smoking wild oats—not good. They caught fish from the boat, built a fire on the beach and slept in their bedrolls. It was a big memory for all because they all raised the money to make it happen, and their enthusiasm made it fun.

All of the children had to go to Catholic Mass every Sunday except for their father. When Bill was twelve he had to go to Confirmation to take the lifetime oath and be confirmed a Catholic. Several weeks before Confirmation day, he had to go to Confession after school. After Confession, a kid named Eugene asked Bill how many "Our Fathers and Hail Marys" he had to say.

"Eight our Fathers and twelve Hail Marys." Bill said.

"Well I did fourteen Our Fathers and twenty Hail Marys," Eugene answered smugly, glaring a wicked worldly glance at Bill.

Bill thought hard that maybe he left some sins out of his own Confession, but it was a fleeting thought. The truth was that, strange as it sounds, in Bill's mind, the competition for sin was on.

At the next Confession, Bill purposefully asked Eugene how many prayers he had to say.

"The same as last time," Eugene answered without looking at Bill.

"Well, I did eighteen Our Fathers and Twenty-five Hail Marys," Bill sharply declared, while silently saying to the Lord,

"Forgive me, Jesus, for lying through my teeth."

Then Bill wondered if lying about sinning was a sin. And if lying that you said a Hail Mary was a sin about a sin that you didn't really do…His brain started to hurt.

Bill's strident retort made Eugene fume in silent, less than holy rage.

On the day of Confirmation, the church made Bill and the other candidates wear vestments, which he thought looked like white dresses. Being a cowboy at heart, he absolutely didn't want anybody to take a picture of him with a dress on, and he sure didn't want any of his Texas Rangers to see him. The Confirmation candidates began walking up the steps to enter the church, hands steepled in an attempted approximation of prayer, heads bowed, and acting holy-like. Suddenly, Eugene fell in line right behind Bill and, as they neared the steps to enter the church, Eugene speared Bill hard in the back with his steeple-folded fingers. Young Bill, with his boxer-trained speed and precision, spun around counter-clockwise on his heels and landed a solid right cross punch right on Eugene's left jaw, and the fight was on. Sister Mary let out a shriek at the sight of two twelve-year-old boys roiling over and under like alligators and thrashing and smashing each other among the sage bushes, and getting their pristine and holy white Confirmation vestments smeared stains.

Sister Mary grabbed Bill by the collar and said, "I saw what you did, Billy O'Brien. You can't go to Confirmation with a sin on your soul. " She sent him home in disgrace.

"All in all, it was a pretty good fight," Bill thought to himself while trying to be sad. He was secretly glad he didn't have to go to Confirmation, but he dare not say.

His mother, who had to stay home to care for one of her boys who was sick, was in the kitchen doing the dishes when he finally got home.

She asked, "How was Confirmation, Bill? Sit down and tell me all about it."

Bill bowed his head saying, "I didn't make it."

It was as if the light had been instantly pulled out of Mother's heart. It was only then Bill realized he was in big trouble, and his tears started flowing down like rain. It wasn't being tossed out of Confirmation that bothered him. It was that he saw his mother was hurt and deeply disappointed.

In The Shedd, Bill looked at me sadly, with his eyes actually brimming with moisture and gravely said, "Real cowboys would never, ever do anything to hurt their mother."

Things weren't quite the same for a couple of years after that. Somehow, the toasters didn't work well, so when the toast was burned, Bill would be the first to have it served to him

"Cowboys like burned toast, don't they Bill?" his mother would say, still hurt from her son's incident.

Being a cowboy, he would answer, "We sure do, ma'am. Blacker the better."

Well, that statement didn't help much, either. He could also see that by not being a confirmed Catholic, his standing in the family was, as he put it "at the bottom of the litter."

BILL'S TRAPLINES AND WILL ROGERS

America in the mid-1930s was still enduring record levels of unemployment, widespread homelessness, hunger and loss of farms and homes. To earn money, Mother kept sharpening her skills as a, what you would call today, a house flipper. She and Father sold the family's Bristol Drive and bought another home at Medio Drive about three miles from Will Rogers State Park. It turned out to be a great home. There was a vacant lot next door that was full of wild oats just like the hills behind Tigertail Road.

The chaparral covering Brentwood hills was teeming with wildlife. After the family moved into the new home, Bill bought a book on trap lines and started a series of trap lines to catch small animals. Eventually, his lines stretched several miles through the canyons. Having sold his successful Saturday Evening Post magazine route and his at-home car wash business, he still needed to earn some money to help support the O'Brien family. After trapping, skinning, salting, and stretching out the animals on stretcher racks at home, Bill would leave the skins to dry out. He then batched them up in bundles and mailed them to the Hudson Bay Company in Illinois.

It took months for Bill to get paid, but after the first checks came in, the cash flow got pretty regular. He kept buying more traps and moving his trap lines farther down into the heavily wooded vegetation. Bill learned an important lesson about conservation and respect for nature. He learned to keep moving into new canyons so he wouldn't clean everything out in one canyon and have nothing to trap the next year. The skins brought pretty good money if they were skinned properly and didn't have holes in them. Bobcat skins brought in four dollars, coyotes, raccoons, and grey-fox skins earned him two dollars each, and possum fifteen cents. He also caught live rattlesnakes along his trap lines and sold them to Hollywood movie studios for three dollars each if they were over three feet long.

For relaxation after a hard day of trapping, Bill set up a coarse but functioning jungle vine swinging system, a series of ropes, cables, hoses, and bound-together Eucalyptus vines. He wanted to be like his favorite Tarzan movie star, Johnny Weissmuller. Bill's jungle vines, while not as graceful and visually pleasing as Tarzan's vines, were still quite functional, and young Bill could actually swing down and up Topanga Canyon.

Bill adopted a Redtick Coon dog that following him home one day. "Queenie," as Bill called him, turned out to be a great hound and a terrific help in the trap line business. His trap line business was thriving. But Bill realized he could not be a real cowboy if he did not have a real horse. So he bought a buckskin horse, paying sixty dollars for him including the saddle, and named him Buck. Buck wasn't much to look at. Bill says his head took two thirds of the space between his ears and the ground. But Buck had a ground-eating jog, meaning he could eat up the miles, and he got Bill around much faster than walking. With trusty old Buck, Bill could set the traps even further out and eventually he had over thirty traps. As the trap lines grew miles longer, so did Bill's income, which taught him the value of expanding your territory. Almost every Friday right after school, Bill, Buck, and Queenie left on business, and they would often camp out in the canyons until very early Monday.

He was making more money than his older brother who had a full time job as a soda jerk pouring malt shakes and earning about one-thousand dollars per year. When Bill missed Catholic Mass, which was often, Mother never said anything because she knew he would give her most of the money. Bill didn't think it was a sin missing Mass anyway, because he was never confirmed as a Catholic and he was helping support the family. After all, he reasoned, he believed in God and he worshiped in his way in the wide open spaces.

As a kid running his trap line in the canyons of Los Angeles, one summer Bill met the cowboy humorist, Will Rogers. Will was a top calf roper and had a ranch home and roping arena just north of Sunset Boulevard at the mouth of one of the canyons near where Bill lived. So one day, when young Bill was trapping on weekends and returning home with his catch, Will Rogers decided to let Bill help him practice roping and turning the calves out with him.

"If you'll let me open your gate, you may gain an extra second or two on your time," Bill persuasively announced to Will Rogers.

The celebrity cowboy columnist agreed, and Bill O'Brien jumped on top of Will Roger's gate with all the energy he could muster, and he became Will Roger's gate keeper for the summer.

Trapping season always faded in the springtime, so it was the perfect time for Bill to join the family for a trip to Clear Lake. It was the last summer to visit their favorite destination. Sister Jane was now in University High School. She was involved in drama and had many leading roles in the senior plays even before she was a senior. Her talent as an aspiring actress was obvious. Brother Jim enrolled in New Mexico Military Institute where the O'Brien boy's maternal grandfather, Captain Murray, had taught history, mathematics, band and polo.

Before leaving on vacation in Clear Lake, Mother insisted Bill find a good home for Buck, the buckskin horse and sell him, because there was no one to take care of him while they gone for the summer. After a half-hearted protest, Bill gave in to his mother's advice, and he found a good home and sold his buckskin horse and saddle earning him one hundred dollars profit. Bill learned that if you take care of what you own, you may be able to sell it at a profit.

Even through the Depression days, Father still owned a water company and some real estate at Clear Lake Park. The Clear Lake Water Company brought Father a little money, but he often said that, "It was a crummy business having to deal with people who wouldn't, or couldn't, pay." Father had figured out a way to pump water out of the lake into a tank on the hill, filter it, and sell it to the houses on the water's edge. He had a manager to maintain the system full-time, which included paying the power bill and making collections. That is all it took to run the company but collecting the money from the people was the downer. Later in life, older brother Jim looked at his father's accounting and found out that Father was worth a million and a half dollars in 1929 and four years later, in 1933, ended up forty thousand dollars in debt. Rather than declare bankruptcy, Father negotiated a deal to pay off the debt over ten years without interest. It was hard on him but taking bankruptcy was unthinkable. Bill said in a later day that, "I am forever proud of my father. It was a lesson to remember the rest of my life—always honor your debts, and stay out of debt unless the reward is greater than the risk."

Their last summer at Clear Lake was one to remember. Jane was a good athlete and, as usual, went horseback riding, swimming and hung out with all the cute, athletic boys. She still liked to swim the three miles across the lake. Bill was now brave enough to dive into the water from the second level of the high dive. He wanted to swim across the lake like Jane did, but Mother only allowed it if brothers Jim and Don rowed a skiff along him. Bill made it across, and a farmer watching on the other side was so impressed that he gave the boys a big basket of delicious peaches to take home.

The family returned home with a lot of summer left. Since Don and Bill loved the beach, they would often take the San Vicente trolley or hitchhike to the Santa Monica beach. Those years it was easy to hitchhike because everyone was struggling to survive and they were sensitive to help those in need, especially young kids. The O'Brien boys became excellent body surfers far away from the Santa Monica Pier because there were no waves inside the breakwater.

FISHERMAN BILL AND FARMERS MARKET

Young Bill loved Santa Monica Pier. He was fascinated with the working fishermen, and the berths at the docks where rich people could store their boats. He wanted to be a part of the Santa Monica pier lifestyle, so he bought a punt, an eight-foot, flat-bottomed boat, squared at both ends, at the right price. That started a whole new business —fishing for halibut. Bill still had his great skinning knife from the trap line business.

"That was the best hunting knife," he often said. "That knife, some line, fishing hooks and a boat was all a true fisherman needed."

For the first few days, he caught mackerel, which was great fun, but nobody around the neighborhood would pay enough, or people simply refused to buy it.

"That is an awfully bony fish," customers would complain as Bill went door to door offering his catch of the day.

As Bill was walking by the pier, he saw an older man. His white hair, beard and skin were soaked by the salt and seasoned by the sun.

"You look like a real fisherman," Bill said.

He was always willing to start a conversation and was eager to learn from those with more experience about things Bill was interested in.

The old man looked at him and smiled, "Yes, I been at it since about your age."

"Do you have any advice for me where I can catch fish?" Bill asked respectfully.

The old man pointed into the sea, beyond the pier. "There is a big hole about a mile and a half out. It's where lots of bottom feeding halibut can be caught."

"That is where the Star of India is," Bill responded.

"No, not that far, about a quarter mile before that."

"Thank you sir," Bill said as he shook the old man's hand.

The Star of India was a masted schooner anchored offshore and there was gambling and drinking because they were outside America's legal three-mile coastline limit.

Bill made a business deal with the Captain Wolfe, the skipper of the Star of India to polish the ships brass while his punt was being towed to that fishing hole that the old fisherman told him about. Getting back after fishing was easy because there was always an onshore afternoon breeze. Bill was equipped with a box of big hooks, a roll of strong twine, two bricks to anchor each end of the set line to prevent drift, and two large orange blocks of cork to float at each end of the set-line.

The old fisherman had told Bill that, to start fishing for Halibut, he had to chum for Mackerel, meaning to throw out bits of smaller fish to attract the Mackerel. Mackerel go into a feeding frenzy around chum and, with a barb-less hook on a short bamboo pole, Bill could get plenty of bait in short order. When he caught the Mackerel, he cut it into chunks, and set the chunks on the 125 hooks of his set line. After that it was easy fishing for Halibut. Sometimes he caught too many Halibut, so he had to throw some back. Bill was less than four foot eight inches tall, and he was limited to how much Halibut he could carry in the gunnysack.

Selling the fish around his neighborhood was easy because customers could see they were freshly caught. Ever mindful of keeping costs down, Bill always stored his punt in different bins, hoping the Harbor Master would lose track of how many days it was stored so he wouldn't charge storage fees.

Bill usually got to the Santa Monica pier around four-thirty in the morning to get an early start. One Sunday morning, he could see flashing Coast Guard lights flashing all over the Star of India. He skipped fishing that day and rowed his punt over just to see what was happening. The Coast Guard were throwing slot machines and heavy card tables overboard. It was a regular raid, just like those police raids on gangster hideouts in the movies.

His skipper friend, a large, middle-aged man who always wore his blue captain's suit and white hat, had already taken his passengers ashore. A tall, well-built guy in a black suit and crew-cut, was standing on the gangway and told Bill to come along side. Bill figured he wanted to get off that schooner and go ashore but Bill was afraid that he might dump him overboard and take over his punt. Bill didn't do it. If he had asked him nicely instead of telling him in a commanding voice, he might have thought differently.

Another time, Bill decided to row to Catalina Island. It was over forty miles away but he thought he could make it there because it didn't look that far. When he was about five miles offshore of Catalina Island, a Coast Guard cutter ship came alongside the little punt and hailed him on the loudspeaker.

"Where are you going," the Coast Guard captain demanded with a stern voice.

"Catalina Island," Bill yelled back respectfully, while trying to sound like an experienced fisherman.

"Get aboard now. We are going to tow your punt back to Santa Monica Pier," the captain ordered.

Even though Bill did not understand why, he obeyed the

officer. On the way back to the pier he was thinking, "How could they do that? This is a free country. They didn't even give me a choice."

He could see what Father meant when he said the government was acting like Big Brother, making Americans do what was best for them whether they liked it or not. Bill concluded the Coast Guard captain was only doing his job and anyway he had no choice, so he thanked the captain for his service.

Summer was about over, and it seemed the Halibut were not as hungry and the bony Mackerel were not biting as they had before. Bill was ready to move on to different adventures. He made a deal with the Harbor Master to let him leave his little square punt in a corner upside down for the winter, if he paid for a new license plate in advance. Since The Star of India lost gambling privileges, Mr. Wolfe, the schooner's captain, was going to sail her to San Diego, and he was looking for a crew. Bill wanted the job however, to do that, he had to take three days off from his eighth grade classes at University High School. But sailing with the Star of India was a once in a lifetime adventure and Bill, along with his friend Harold, signed on to be part of the crew.

Bill imagined that the job would involve the two boys climbing aloft, hoisting anchor, and unfurling sails. But their sailing dreams were crushed when he and Harold were suddenly below deck, pumping bilge water in the dank air, all the way to San Diego. Every so often the captain would open the hatch and gruffly bark, "Keep pumping kids." With all that pounding in the surging sea, the boys were losing ground on the pumping bilge, and losing their appetite for the sailing way of life.

As soon as they docked in San Diego Harbor, Bill and Harold jumped right off the bow of The Star of India and swam ashore to the sandy beach. With one regretful glance back at the old schooner, the boys looked at each other and agreed that this job was not for them. They walked to the highway and hitchhiked back home to Brentwood. They never did get to collect their pay, but they were plenty thankful they made it on shore alive. Still, it was an adventure, after all.

Back home on Medio Drive, Bill had made friends with some Japanese kids whom he met in his history class. After school, they invited Bill to go to another class to learn Japanese history, Jiu-Jitsu, and how to make crystal radio sets. As a trained boxer, Bill was fascinated with Jiu-Jitsu. He learned how to make a crystal radio with the help of his pal, Johnny Kitsue. It was amazing that they could talk to each other a mile away from their homes. Johnny's family had a prosperous Lima bean farm on Wilshire and Sepulveda Boulevard. Nobody seemed to care if you were white, black, brown, yellow, or red. In the glorious meritocracy of adolescence, a pal was a pal and a jerk was a jerk.

Bill loved to go with Mother to the new Farmers Market in Los Angeles. Opened in 1934, the sizable Farmers' Market quickly became the must-see destination for out-of-town visitors, area residents, and Hollywood movie stars. Eventually, Bill landed a job at the Farmers' Market on weekends hauling groceries for the movie stars and local residents. He was given a cart and the short on-the job training advice, Go help out, and just started asking everyone he met if he could carry their groceries to their car. When he did, they gave him a tip. Bill always saw plenty of movie stars at the Farmers' Market because they saw it was the in thing to do. Bill always liked to help the horror film star, Boris Karloff, and plenty of other movie stars that he recognized but didn't know their names, unless they were in the cowboy movies.

Usually during lunch, the gang of carryout boys would have their lunch behind a fence, out of sight from the customers. The older boys would tell off-color jokes. One of the jokes Bill remembers went like this:

One day Will Rogers and Mae West both spotted a fifty-cent silver coin in the sawdust at the outdoor market. They scrambled to reach down and pick it up, but both Mae West and Will Rogers grabbed it at the same time and held on tightly to each side of the silver coin. While raising his thin wiry frame back up in victory, Will Rogers bumped his head into Mae West's bosom.

"Mae," he said, "If your heart is as soft as your bosom, you'll let me keep that fifty cents."

"Will, if your member down there is as hard as your head, then come up and see me sometime.'"

Well, the boys all laughed but Bill knew better than to tell that joke at home, especially to his Dad.

One Sunday, before going to his job at the Farmers Market, Bill went to see the famous evangelist, Amy Semple McPherson, preach a sermon in Beverly Hills. Bill was curious about what all the fuss was about this female preacher who was once greeted at Los Angeles train station by fifty thousand people. From what he heard, this lady was amazing because she got people to pay just to hear her preach.

The church was packed that day. Amy Semple McPherson introduced two men dressed in flowing white robes, and she told everyone in the church that these men were Saints." She said it so many times and so seriously that people got to thinking, "Maybe they are Saints. Then she would preach about the Lord and how good He was. She would raise her voice and lower it and raise it again, by saying Praise the Lord.

After a while, Bill got the message about how the lady preacher worked the crowd, so he started to leave.

Then the lady preacher cried out, "Now everybody who is going to contribute a dollar right now for the Lord's work, please stand up."

Suddenly, the organ started playing The Star-Spangled Banner and, of course, being Americans, everybody stood up. Just then, the Saints passed long wooden poles with clothes pins nailed to them. The least you could donate was a one-dollar bill. They waggled those ten-foot poles in front of people until they were shamed into clipping a bill onto the clothespin.

All eyes were on the electrifying Amy Semple McPherson, but Bill still had seen enough. He said to himself, "What a racket, I wish I'd thought of that idea."

CULTURAL DIVERSITY

Bill was doing well at University High, called Uni Hi, "It was a darn good school," he would always say.

There were unusual classes for the time, like Social Studies, Music Appreciation and Writing, as well as some practical ones like Carpentry, Print Shop and Typing. Later to be called vocational classes, those classes were designed to help get the students a job when they graduated. Bill liked history, Spanish, Math, Gym and Drama.

A big day in Spanish class was when they went on a field trip to Olivera Street. It was a real eye opener to see how Mexican-Americans were getting along in life in Los Angeles. They always tried to do their best, even though many had so little, and they remained polite and thankful. No matter what, the Mexicans dressed their kids in colorful clean clothes. That deeply impressed Bill who ever since then, always made sure his clothes and his appearance were impeccable. Once, Bill bought three Mexican jumping beans for a nickel. He was curious about how they worked, so he cracked one open and discovered, to his surprise, that it was a little worm in there wiggling around that made them move. Bill was pretty good at boxing for his weight and was getting better at competitive rope climbing and floor exercises with the gym team. Uni High was a great experience because of the excellent teachers and the diversity of kids. About a third of the students were Mexicans, a third Japanese, and the other third was split between blacks and whites. Bill said that racial problems were not so harsh and divisive as they are today.

Bill loved his teachers. Mrs. Kent taught Spanish and was always kind and helpful. She and Mr. Jimenez, a young Spanish man, taught Math and upper-grade Spanish. Bill was Uni High class president one year and named his class, "The Mohicans."

There was a movie in Westwood called The Last of the Mohicans, and since Bill's was the last class to go completely though school from the sixth to the twelve grade, that name stuck.

Bill was too small for football, not tall enough for basketball, and not strong enough to join the Varsity gym team. He decided to become a cheerleader, or "Yell Leader" as they were called, and they were almost always men at the time. He attended the UCLA football games, not to enjoy the game but to learn how the college Yell Leaders did their new cheers and card stunts. Card stunts involve handing out to volunteer spectators sitting in a section stacks of ten to thirty colored cardboard cards per person. Each stack is organized so that, on the Yell Leader's cue, each card is turned over, one at a time. The result is that the stadium can read large blocks of text or colored logos, based on the participation of the group of volunteers. The stunt involves a high degree of organizational ability, and concentration on the part of the Yell Leader. Bill later went on to be a Yell Leader at University of Arizona and his early exposure to this tradition helped him rally the football crowds into a frenzy.

Ever the entrepreneur, Bill also thought that he could get a job selling hot dogs or Cokes in the football stadium. Helping set up the college cheerleaders with their card stunts got him in free, and he applied for the vendor job. Cokes sold for a dime but he got to keep a nickel. The distributor made him pay a nickel for the Cokes first, so he learned the principal of "It takes money to make money."

One game, Bill watched a black UCLA player throw a Hail Mary pass almost eighty yards to another black player. Bill realized then that African Americans, which they called Blacks back then, were superior athletes. His gym coach said their athleticism and sportsmanship would one day open the eyes of sports fans across America, enabling Blacks to play sports along with white guys.

Bill's adventurous spirit always had him searching for new escapades. One time he found a gangster's hideout with a bank safe blown open under a Sumac tree. There was also a Catholic Chalice, a ciborium cup, and some gold plates left in this hideout. Bill brought the gangster's loot home and his mother called the cops. The police quickly arrived with a Los Angeles Times reporter and Bill proudly showed them the gangster's hideout where the safe was hidden. The police took all the rest of the stolen goods with them and returned it to the church.

Mother loved to see Bill's picture in the paper and she took Bill to Monsignor Connelly at the Santa Monica Catholic Church. The monsignor gave Bill a ten dollar bill. Before he could say thanks, Mother quickly took the money and deposited it in the church box, said a prayer, and lit a candle. Bill thought that was okay, but on second thought, he sure could have used the dough. Mother taught the kids a lot about values, sacrifice, and acting on your beliefs.

One time, Father drove the four kids, on the family Model B Ford, and they went car camping. They wanted to see how the work was progressing on the new dam in the Southern Nevada portion on the Colorado River.

The dam had been called many names, both for logistical and for political reasons. The names included Boulder Canyon Project, Black Canyon, and Boulder Dam. Almost exactly five years earlier September 17, 1930, Secretary of the Interior Ray Lyman Wilbur, under President Herbert Hoover, went to the dam site to drive the spike marking the project's official start. Being from Washington, he thought nothing of wearing his three-piece suit, and he was sweating profusely through his seasonally inappropriate wool suit. Wilbur announced, without authorization from the President or the Congress, "I have the honor and privilege of giving a name to this new structure. In Black Canyon, under the Boulder Canyon Project Act, it shall be called the Hoover Dam."

Wilbur's unofficial dedication was much criticized by the public and the press. The country was still suffering through a crippling Depression that many blame President Hoover for. It went back to being called Boulder Dam when Hoover lost his reelection. Then, on April 30, 1947, President Harry S. Truman signed the resolution and restored the name "Hoover Dam" to the structure.

After they visited the dam, Father and kids visited desert rock shops to buy some rose quartz. Young Bill, ever the sharp businessman, was able to purchase the rose quartz, but only after he haggled the shop owner down to a fair price. Father was proud of how Bill had turned into a capable businessman.

SISTER JANE, THE HOLLYWOOD MOVIE STAR

Finally, there was great news for the O'Brien family. In the mid-1930s, the Hollywood movie studio system was in full swing, and many new movie stars were being discovered. Among them, Bill's sister Jane, landed the lead role in a play called, "Green Grow the Lilacs," thanks to her work at Jean Muir's Acting School in Hollywood. The play was later called, "Oklahoma."

Top American film producer, Hal Wallis, who produced "Casablanca," "The Maltese Falcon," "True Grit" and other hits, saw the play and immediately signed Jane O'Brien to a movie contract with Warner Brothers. The famous Hollywood actress, Bette Davis, who in her career won two Academy Awards and nine Oscar nominations, took an interest in Jane for her acting ability, obvious charm, and social graces. Jane became Bette Davis' protégé, appearing in movies with her. Before Jane signed with Warner Brothers, the studio made her change her stage name to "Jane Bryan," to avoid offending famous Warner Brother's movie actor Pat O'Brien. Father, being a very proud Irishman, took great umbrage to the name change, but Mother outvoted him and the name stuck.

One Saturday afternoon in 1938, the teenage boys from the Texas Rangers climbed the fence to Pat O'Brien's house and were swimming naked in his pool. Suddenly, a startled Pat O'Brien appeared by the pool, with his arms folded and wearing a long white bathrobe. Bill was very embarrassed and told Mr. O'Brien it was all his fault because he heard that he had gone to Hawaii. The boys quickly exited the pool, dressed hurriedly, and started climbing back over the wall.

Pat O'Brien called out to Bill and told him to return. The movie actor gave Bill his business card and told him to hand-deliver it to the cast director the following Saturday at Universal Studios. He told young Bill that auditions were being held that Saturday for the lead role in the upcoming movie, The Adventures of Tom Sawyer. Bill took his bike that Saturday morning on the long haul up the steep Cahuenga Canyon, but he was determined to get there. There must have been two hundred kids trying out for Tom Sawyer. Bill had four auditions and it came down to a choice between him and a kid named Tommy Kelly. Bill thought things were going great for him during the final audition until, in the scene where Bill had to walk hand-in-hand with Ann Gillis, as Tom Sawyer's gal, Becky Thatcher, that Bill's movie dream came crashing to a finale.

"Sorry, Bill, we're going with Tommy Kelly for the role," director Norman Taurog told him with a patient but tired voice. "Bill, you did extremely well and you have natural acting ability, but you are about three inches shorter than the lead actress Ann Gillis. That doesn't look good on the screen."

"Well, maybe by the time you got down to actually making the movie I would grow some more." Bill tried to convince the director.

Director Taurog laughed softly but it didn't do any good.

"Not too shabby for my first audition," Bill said to me with a humorous smile in The Shedd.

Thanks to Pat O'Brien's courtesy toward Bill during their chance meeting at the movie actor's mansion, Bill remained friends with Pat and his Irish wife for rest of his life. Bill always thanked Pat for his recommendation for the part in Tom Sawyer as it was a great experience.

Sister Jane was making more movies and she was getting paid a lot of money. She wanted to give her father a car as a Christmas present. Her mother had a friend who was a car dealer in Phoenix and would give her a good deal. Jane wanted to take one of her brothers with her, and Bill was the lucky one. The six-hour drive through Southern California's greenery and Arizona's desert with Jane, one of his favorite people, was a memorable one. In Phoenix they stayed at the upscale Westward Ho hotel, a favorite place for Hollywood movie stars, business tycoons, and celebrities.

While Jane was sunning herself on a lounge chair, Bill was doing flips off of the diving board. He shared the diving board with a tall, broad-shouldered, good-looking guy doing flips as well. Bill wanted to show off, so he did a one-and-a-half flip. To his surprise, the broad-shouldered guy did two flips. That was impressive because Bill had never seen that before. His name was Justin Dart, and Bill learned later he was a successful Walgreen's drug store executive from Chicago who later founded the national Rexall Drug store chain. Justin introduced himself to Bill and complimented the young man on his form.

Bill introduced Justin to his sister Jane, and the three had lunch together. After lunch, Justin invited Jane and Bill to the rodeo arena at the Biltmore Resort Hotel.

Bill saw Justin Dart put an additional hundred dollars into the betting pot for the bronc riding event. Doc Pardee, who was a famous Arizona cowboy and rodeo announcer said Justin Dart's name over the loud speaker, and the new bet created even more betting and sweetened the pot.

As they all said their goodbyes, Bill was very pleased when Justin asked Bill if he could see Jane the next time he was in

California. Receiving Bill's permission, Justin and Jane made plans to see each other in Los Angeles in a few weeks. After that, Jane and Justin Dart dated cross-country for months, and Bill got to see more of him on his visits to Los Angeles.

Bill and Jane drove the new car back home to Los Angeles. Jane wrapped the car all the way around with a giant red ribbon, a huge bow, and an oversize card saying "Merry Christmas Poppy!" Their dad was really surprised and seemed so proud on Christmas morning when he walked outside. After a decade of struggle and economic hardship for the O'Briens, it was a great family moment to remember, full of love and lots of hugs.

As Jane's movie career skyrocketed, many famous Hollywood movie stars came over to the O'Brien home to take Jane out on a date. Young Bill would entertain Jane's celebrity dates until Jane came downstairs. Eddie Albert, gave Bill his old guitar one evening while dating Jane and showed him how to play it. One time, Bill greeted actor Ronald Reagan at the door. To keep him occupied, Bill made a bet with him to toss a silver dime and make it stay on the top of the long beam on the ceiling in the living room. The person whose dime stayed up on the beam would win the dime. Of course Bill had practiced this act with other movie stars who came over to date Jane, so Bill usually won the bet. It was a fun way to pass the time while they waited for Jane to come down. Jane was a real Irish beauty and a true Hollywood movie star. She would have a great future ahead of her, Bill thought, wherever that future might lead.

ECHOS OF WAR AND MARRIAGE OF
JANE AND JUSTIN

By the end of 1938, the world was in collective anxiety.

The drums of war echoed around the globe and one of the darkest moments in history was about to corrupt the conscience of mankind.

Japan had been fighting China.

German military mobilizes.

British Prime Minister Chamberlain appeases Hitler at Munich.

British fleet mobilizes; Civilian evacuations begin from London.

Nazis invade Poland and then take Czechoslovakia

Britain, France, Australia and New Zealand declare war on Germany.

British Royal Air Force attacks the German Navy.

German troops cross the Vistula River in Poland.

Canada declares war on Germany; Battle of the Atlantic begins.

Soviets invade Poland. Nazis and Soviets divide up Poland.

German U-boats attack merchant ships in the Atlantic.

Battle of Britain begins. Soviets take Lithuania, Latvia and Estonia.

Italians occupy British Somaliland in East Africa. German bombing offensive against airfields and factories in England.

First German air raids on Central London. First British air raid on Berlin.

Nazis invade Denmark, Norway, France, Belgium, Luxembourg and the Netherlands; Winston Churchill becomes British Prime Minister.

Germans bomb Paris and demolished the city.

By 1940, a full scale global assault, the most destructive conflict in history, cost more money, damaged more property, killed more people, and caused more geographical changes than any other war in history.

In America, the economy was still struggling ten years after Black Tuesday, but the nation was expanding its military might. Industrial activity was slightly below the level of ten years earlier. In the summer of 1939, approximately nine million persons were unemployed in the United States, a 17% unemployment rate.

Since Jane's movie career was going great, she frequently asked brother Bill to come as her chaperone. Consequently, he was attending many parties in Hollywood and Beverly Hills and got a taste of the Hollywood life style. He spent much of his time at the Santa Monica Beach club and loved to body surf. It was the good life, and why not?

During the Depression, he had worked his whole childhood in his many businesses, so why not have a little fun? But his family was wondering what he was going to do with his life. Mummy Dart, Justin's mother, was visiting from Evanston, Illinois and she came over to see Bill's mother, Irene. The ladies were upset about Bill's playboy lifestyle and when he came home that evening, they told him that he was nothing but a playboy. Bill's feelings were hurt. But, ever resourceful and action-oriented, he took their criticism to heart. Bill took a summer job that Justin Dart told him about working in a New

Jersey manufacturing plant, assembling and selling Aeroil weed burners. It would get Bill out of California and earn him some money for college.

The Aeroil weed burners could be used it to incinerate and destroy weeds, seeds, and roots; you could disinfect poultry and livestock quarters as well.

Bill was a born salesman and he was doing well selling Aeroil weed burners, but after a semester he discovered the product was now being sold at many department and hardware stores everywhere. He didn't see much future in that job. The lesson was don't compete with the big boys unless you have a direct pipeline to the customer, or at least a unique offer nobody else can match.

Jane was more interested in building her movie career and making movies than dating movie stars. And she had fallen very much in love with Justin Dart. Jane had to make a choice between her Hollywood movie career and love, so Jane consulted her mentor and friend Bette Davis.

Without the slightest hesitation, Bette Davis told Jane, "Follow your heart and marry Justin Dart."

Jane and Justin married on New Year's Eve, December 31, 1939, in Chicago. Always a devoted daughter, Jane paid for the round-trip train fare from California to Chicago to bring the entire O'Brien family to the wedding. After the wedding, Bill saw the newlyweds quickly rush to the hotel service elevator. Bill found out later they did this to dodge the mob of business and society reporters gathered in the lobby. Bill took a walk alone around the block before going to the hotel. In the freezing snow of Chicago on winterly New Year's Eve, it was the coldest, windiest experience he ever had, especially since he was walking around in his brand new Panama suit, his only suit, and no overcoat. That hot shower in the hotel room was one of the greatest luxuries of his life at the time.

When Jane walked away from Warner Brothers, she had appeared in almost twenty films. Bette Davis was right. Jane followed her heart, gave up her career, and married Justin Dart.

The Darts lived in Chicago and Boston before moving to Los Angeles in the 1940s. The couple built a house in Bel Air and had a weekend home near Palm Springs. Jane knew Ronald Reagan because they had been in several movies together. She introduced Justin Dart to Ronald Regan and his first wife, actress Jane Wyman. Their friendship lasted for the rest of their lives, but it took both men some getting used to.

Of Ronald Reagan, Justin Dart once said, ""'At the time Ronald Reagan was a rabid Democrat. The night we first met, we fought like cats and dogs. Jane warned me not to talk politics with him."

Later on, in 1945, Justin Dart took over the struggling Rexall Drugstore chain and built it eventually into Dart-Kraft, a food and consumer products empire. Seven years later, in 1952, after Reagan married his second wife, Nancy, Justin Dart joined Reagan's inner circle, becoming the informal leader of Ronald Regan's Kitchen Cabinet. That group persuaded Regan to run for governor of California and later, for president.

On the Christmas school vacation of 1940, while still in high school, Bill had a great opportunity to become a real cowboy. Jane and Justin Dart invited the whole family to the JD Ranch in Rimrock, Arizona. The big event was that Jane's longtime friend and mentor, actress Bette Davis, was getting married to Arthur Farnsworth on New Year's Eve at the ranch that Justin and Jane Dart owned. The date was exactly one year after Jane and Justin Dart got married. Built in 1870, the historic property was the site of the popular Quail's Nest, now called The Ranch

House Restaurant, which opened a year earlier in 1939. A favorite watering hole during the golden age of Hollywood, the ranch entertained movie stars like Frank Sinatra, John Wayne, and Clark Gable.

It was a great trip for Bill since he met several important people, among them, Justin's mother, Laura Case Whitlock Dart, or "Mummy Dart," as she liked to be called. Bill got to drive her enormous new Cadillac. The car felt so safe and heavy. Young Bill, then seventeen years old, felt very important driving it. Mummy Dart constantly reminded Bill to keep it under seventy miles per hour. Her calm voice and confidence was quite a different approach to what he was used to. Bill also met Port Parker, a local cattle rancher who was building an airport for Mr. Dart on a square butte not far from Rimrock. At last, Bill met a real cowboy in Port Parker, who was tall, lean, wiry, and spoke in a slow, gentling voice that seemed to calm man and beast alike.

Bill worked most of his Christmas vacation for Port, moving big boulders and removing brush with Arizona cowboys, as Port ran the bulldozer, and that was plenty of fun for him.

With all that dazzling glamor, and effusive movie stars gathering for Bette Davis' wedding, of course it was going to be spectacular. But Bill O'Brien was far more interested in working side-by-side with real Arizona cowboys like Port Parker and his ranch hands. One afternoon, after a hard day's work, they drove to Montezuma's Castle, a thousand-year-old Indian dwelling built ninety-feet above a sheer limestone cliff by the Verde River. The building of the castle began in 1100 AD by the Sinagua Indians and it took over three-hundred years to build it. The name, "Montezuma's Castle," is romantic, but completely inaccurate. More like a pre-Columbian high-rise apartment complex, the cliff dwellings were built years before the Aztec emperor was born and has absolutely no connection to the Montezuma.

Bill, Port Parker, and his new cowboy pals got to crawl inside the adobe house in the open cave, and they treated the incredible Indian ruins with respect. Years later, from 1951 onward, visitors are no longer allowed to go inside the cliff dwellings, so Bill had a rare privilege to see it.

After the New Year's wedding they returned to Brentwood. As long as they lived at home, brothers Bill and Don still had to go to Mass with their mother. Even though Bill never became an official Catholic, on account of that fistfight he had on the way to Confirmation, church was mandatory, "and I mean it," Mother always told the boys. Father never attended church but had his private time with his Maker, and older brother Jim was away studying at the New Mexico Military Institute. The priest always talked in Latin and Bill never understood a word, and he never understood why. Later in life he would say that, "You had to sit there until it was time to stand up, then kneel, and then sit awhile. I just didn't get it, but I knew it was good for you and I still remember every required prayer in the book. I think the best thing the priest taught me was to have a conscience. If you keep your conscience clean and believe in God, then you will probably cross the Great Divide in good shape."

RUNNING AWAY TO BE A COWBOY

With one semester of high school left. Bill needed a change of scenery. He decided to leave home shortly after returning from Bette Davis' wedding at the Dart's Ranch. He wanted to become a cowboy, and live the life of the Old West. Bill's great friend, Marshall Riddick, who was later a Navy pilot, but was to be shot down in the South Pacific, took Bill to Long Beach where the freight trains pulled out heading east. Bill practiced running next to a slow-moving train and throwing his saddle and bedroll on a freight car. Then he would jump on and off as it started slowly gaining speed. It was so easy, and the hobos did it all the time in need for shelter. So one dark night, Bill quietly said goodbye to his brothers and sister, and Marshall dropped him off at the train yard. Wearing his cowboy hat, white shirt, red bandana, cowboy boots, and Levis, and carrying his saddle, bedroll, bag of beef jerky, some bread and a canteen, Bill ran alongside a slow-moving freight train. He found an open freight car and jumped on.

The train left Los Angeles, passed Palm Springs, and came to a stop in Indio, California, and just sat there. The trip was exhilarating, but after a few hours sitting on a freight car in the desert morning sun, Bill had enough. "Cowboys don't just sit around," he thought to himself. Bill scanned the horizon past the Indio train yard and spied a real rodeo happening right there in the distance. So he jumped off the freight car, took his cowboy gear and hiked over to watch.

He was fascinating by all the rodeo action, the sights, sounds, smells, and cowboy lingo. He picked up new words and sayings by listening intently to the rodeo announcers and practiced getting the accent right. He learned words like: Arm Jerker: A horse or bull that can really buck. Broke Horse: A horse with some training is a broke horse; a green-broke horse is partially educated; a well-broke horse is highly educated, noble, and dignified. Earring down: subduing a wild horse by twisting its ears. Fishing: When the roper misses the cow, then flips the rope, and turns it into a legal catch. Freight Trained: Getting run over in the rodeo arena by a huge beast going flat out. Hat Bender: A horse or bull that doesn't not buck at all, he just runs around. Definitely not a crowd pleaser. Pulling Leather: Holding onto the saddle horn to keep from getting thrown when a horse is bucking. Considered bad form in rodeo events. Seeing Daylight: When the bucking bronc or bull bucks so hard the cowboy can see daylight between him and the horse. Sunfishing: When a bucking horse stiffly contorts his body in the shape of a crescent Bill also picked up some cowboy wisdom in sayings such as: "Don't squat with yer spurs on." "Always drink upstream from the herd." "Never smack a man who's chewin' tobacco." "Never kick a fresh turd on a hot day." "The only way to drive cattle fast is slowly." "The first thing to do when you get up in the morning is put on your Stetson." Whenever three cowboys are in a truck, the real cowboy sits in the middle seat. He doesn't have to drive, and he doesn't have to get out all the time and open the gate. Bill was impressed by seeing a cowboy who just won prize money, in the saddle bronc event. With all the cowboy swagger and attitude he could muster, Bill sauntered over with his saddle, bedroll, and gear and introduced himself to a cowboy who had just won day money in the bronc riding and Bill asked him, "Great riding out there in the area. My name's Bill O'Brien. Say, could I get a ride to wherever you are going?"

The cowboy looked at the seventeen-year old kid and smiled. "Howdy, Bill. My name's Sid Despain. Sure you can, but first, I'm fixin' to go to the dance hall next door. If'n you're still here by my Chevy pickup truck and rig, when I get back tonight, I'll take ya' with me. Just water and feed my horse until I get back."

Trying hard to contain his enthusiasm, Bill said okay and rolled out his bedroll on the ground next to the driver's side so the cowboy wouldn't forget him when he got back from the dance. It was four o'clock in the morning when Sid came back to his rig and saw Bill camped next to the truck.

Sid was feeling pretty good having won the day money at the rodeo and they took off in the early morning light toward Salome, Arizona. Bill had read about Salome because, when Bill had his Saturday Evening Post magazine route, he always read reprints of the humor columns by Dick Wick Hall, who wrote columns for the magazine. Throwing journalistic integrity to the wind, Dick Wick Hall, just made up outrageously tall tales with no point other than to befuddle and amuse the reader. Hall created a variety of characters for his columns, the most famous being a seven-year-old desert frog that had never learned to swim.

As Bill told me in The Shedd, the frog never learned, "On account of he was a desert frog, so he didn't need to know how to swim!"

To this day, Dick Wick Hall is also credited with naming the town, Salome, inspired by his business partner's wife, Grace Salome Pratt. As Bill O'Brien tells it:

One incredibly hot July afternoon in the early days of the

town's founding, Grace Salome inexplicably took off her shoes and socks in the middle of the town's main street to walk across to the saloon. Why? The heat, discomfort, boredom, who knew? Suddenly, Grace Salome started hopping so violently because of the hot sand, first on one foot then the other, that the townsfolk thought she was merely dancing for joy, for craziness, for whatever.

The name Salome stuck, and Dick Wick Hall, ever the Public Relation expert and co-founder of the town, Salome, made sure of that.

Bill thought Dick Wick Hall's humorous articles were funnier than those of Will Rogers, the famous cowboy and political humorist. But Will Rogers always had a message in his stories, whether it be political, social, economic, or just full of cowboy wisdom.

Sid and Bill drove in Sid's Chevy pickup truck and horse trailer through beautiful northern Arizona, up Yarnell Hill, through Prescott and Mayer, and then winding down Mingus Mountain, past the ghost town, Jerome, to Cottonwood. Sid dropped young Bill off at the Cottonwood general store. The store had a weathered wooden sidewalk that made your boots make that soul-satisfying "clump, clump, clump" sound when you walked on it. Bill thought, "Man, this is really Cowboy Country." He hung around the Cottonwood general store for many hours, asking dozens of cowboys and ranchers for work, trying not to appear desperate, because cowboys don't beg.

It was late on Saturday afternoon when a rancher walked in whom Bill recognized from last Christmas at the Dart's ranch. He was Port Parker that Bill had helped move boulders for the Rimrock Airport when Bette Davis got married on Justin and Jane Dart's ranch. But Port didn't act like he recognized Bill.

Bill O'Brien, sauntered purposefully over and said "Howdy,"

and reminded him that Bill helped Port move all those boulders the year before, and asked if the rancher could use a cowboy.

The tall, lean, Port Parker studied the seventeen-year-old the thin, but wiry, Bill O'Brien with his saddle, bedroll, and gear.

After quite a spell, Port Parker said "We don't need any cowboys in my outfit but if you want to be my chore boy, I'll put you on right now."

Young Bill O'Brien could instantly feel his dreams of being a cowboy come hurtling toward the red Rimrock dirt. Bill must have thought, "How am I going to write home and say I've now made it as a chore boy on an Arizona cattle ranch?"

Bill had only eight bucks in his pocket, so he kept looking Port Parker steadily in the eye, acting like he was thinking over his dozens of job offers.

He finally said, extracting all the enthusiasm he could gather, "I'll take the job."

Port Parker, who later became Chief Cattle Inspector for the State of Arizona, and inventor of the famous Port Parker Saddle, was, indeed, a real honest-to-goodness Arizona cowboy. Being a chore boy on the JD Ranch was the beginning of some of the happiest days of Bill O'Brien's life.

On the JD ranch there was plenty of work to do, like mending fences and mucking out the feed corrals. Bill had to milk the cows every morning and night, collect the eggs, and chop mesquite for the bunkhouse stoves and fireplace. Most important of all, Bill had to personally exercise Dorado, Port's stud horse, every single day, which was pure joy for Bill.

Young Bill was eager to keep his job, even mastering the skill of expertly spreading the horse manure across the hay fields. On Saturday nights Bill and Gordon, Port's head honcho, would go over to the Rimrock School House dance. They would ride a couple of green-broke horses down to the highway, tie them to a Jack Pine tree, and hail any pickup truck going their way. Then, afterwards, they would catch a ride back to their broncs and ride in the pitch-black forest back to the ranch.

The dance was always an outstanding event to look forward to. One Saturday night, Bill was dancing with a very nice looking red-headed girl. She was shorter than Bill, which sure helped his ego.

Just when things were going great, several; truckloads of Civilian Conservation Corps guys swarmed to the Rimrock School House, burst open the door, and barged onto the dance hall floor. Bill thought these CCC boys were different than cowboys. They did make-work programs that President Roosevelt started during the Great Depression, mainly to get Americans back on their feet and instill some pride in them. Bill saw that these guys didn't even clean up for the dance.

As Bill told me in The Shedd, he thought the trouble with this particular gang of boys was that they had no creed, poor manners, and they looked like transients. The Rimrock area cowboys resented the CCC gangs because they were trying to sweet talk the local cowgirls away from them.

Well, one of these guys went up behind Bill, put his hand on Bill's shoulder and told him he was cutting in to dance with "this fine-lookin' filly." That really pissed Bill off and he shouted over his shoulder, "You're not cuttin' in here, mister." The man balled up his fists, glared at Bill and said, "Let's settle this right now." So Bill excused himself from his dancing partner and the two young men went outside to duke it out.

Bill's opponent was a little bit bigger than him, but Bill had a lot more boxing training and maybe was a little bit faster, so it looked like it was going to be a pretty good fight. As they went after each other, they were both getting their licks in, but then another cowboy started shoving one of the new-coming boys, and he shoved back, and pretty soon there was one heck of a brawl in the cloud of red dirt outside the Rimrock School House. Then one of the cowboys hit the guy who Bill was fighting with a small split pine log and knocked him out cold. Bill was impressed, but that wasn't the way he was taught to fight. Still, he seized the opportunity and grabbed the split log, and he started swinging and growling like one of those mountain lions he frequently saw on horseback. Bill's sudden animal-like behavior seemed to scare everyone, including the surprised cowboys, and then the CCC guys started swearing and ran back to their trucks. Bill's pal, Gordon, detached a heavy tailgate from the back of one of the trucks and threw it on top of the guys sitting in the bed of the truck. Bill thought to himself that wasn't fair because those guys had already quit.

As the fleet of fleeing trucks disappeared down the moonlit road, Bill dusted the red dirt off his clothes and went back looking for the red-head, but, sadly, she had already left.

To celebrate their victory, the cowboys went over to a scruffy-looking old timer selling moonshine from the back of his pickup, and they starting pounding down shots of the white lightning. Everyone joined in the ceremony except Gordon, who was a Mormon, and Bill gained a deeper respect and understanding of the Mormon way of life that night. One of the cowboys bought Bill a shot. On his first sip, it was so strong that Bill spilled most of it out while coughing. Gordon just shook his head and smiled at the young cowboy, no longer a boy, not yet a man. Bill recovered and still managed a toast to his fellow cowboys.

Bill figured he could stay on at the JD Ranch forever, but unfortunately it was only for the summer. Towards the end of the summer, his mother drove all the way to Rimrock from Los

Angeles. She marched right into the ranch bunkhouse, grabbed Bill by the ear in front of all the cowboys and ranch hands and said, "You're coming back with me right now to finish high school, and I mean it." That was really humiliating, but Bill could see that she was not going to take "No" for an answer. But, despite the fact that he hopped a freight train to Arizona to become a cowboy, that he didn't tell his parents where he was going, that he never wrote home, and that four years earlier he had been kicked out of Confirmation for fighting and never became a Catholic, Bill finally understood that Mother really did love him.

As they sped off down the Black Canyon Freeway, Bill looked at his mother and realized she had been filled with righteous anger and concern over his educational development. Hers was a justifiable anger that compelled her to rescue this young man from what he thought was his true calling. She knew what the world would soon know—that Bill O'Brien was destined for greatness.

Always a good businessman, Bill had saved his money from his various businesses. So, instead of starting new business, he cracked the books and was able to concentrate on finishing the senior year and the heavy courses at Uni High. It was pretty obvious to Bill that he was going to have to go on to college after graduation; Father was pretty adamant about that. Bill's grades were good enough to go to any college he wanted. He was accepted to Stanford University, thinking he wanted to be a lawyer like his dad, but Father was against that idea.

Father had said "The law profession has lost its high moral calling and true purpose. I tell you that one day you'll even see lawyers running advertisements in newspapers and magazines. Shocking! By the time you get your law degree, lawyers will be more interested in making profits than upholding the law."

Bill loved his dad and wanted to follow his advice about college, but he was still itching to be a real cowboy. In January, 1941, after successfully completing the missing classes he needed to graduate from high school, he hitchhiked back with his cowboy gear to Rimrock, Arizona to get his old chore boy job back. At the JD Ranch, Port Parker took Bill back at the same pay even though the cattle market seemed sluggish. In August Port called in Bill and another ranch hand, a full-blooded Apache Indian, and the cattle business was getting tougher. Port said he had to let one of them go, and it was either him or the Apache Indian. Port decided to let Bill go and keep the Apache Indian.

Bill always believed in the saying, "When the Lord closes one door, another door opens, provided you keep your eyes open and look for it." He packed his gear and his saddle and thanked Port for all he had taught him.

As Bill was hitchhiking out of Rimrock, carrying his saddle, rope, and duffel bag, Chuck McKeen, a cowboy pal he had worked the wild horses with, pulled over in his old pickup truck and said to Bill, "Listen Bill, I'm going to Tucson and enroll at University of Arizona. Why don't you come with me? I've seen you reading all the time. Why not get a college degree now, make a lot of dough, then come back here to Rimrock and buy your own ranch?"

Bill got the message, thanked his pal, and jumped in the truck. Three days later, on account of it was an old truck and broke down a few times, the two cowboys arrived at University of Arizona on September, 1941, three months before the Japanese surprise attack on Pearl Harbor.

Young Bill, destined to be a cowboy.

Bill and his horse.

PEARL HARBOR AND IWO JIMA

On December 7, 1941, two years after Germany invaded Poland, and four years after Japan invaded China, America was ripped out of its isolationism by the surprise attack of Pearl Harbor. Millions of Americans swarmed the military recruiting centers, anxious to enlist and to fight the good fight. Many were too young, or too old, or had family responsibilities.

Two months after the Japanese attack on Pearl Harbor, President Franklin D. Roosevelt authorized the deportation and incarceration to all suspicious people of Japanese descent on the entire West Coast. The FBI quickly began rounding up any suspicious Japanese for internment. None was ever charged with any crime and almost all were simply Japanese community leaders. They were taken away without notice, even though that most families knew nothing about why their men had suddenly disappeared, to where they were taken, or when they would be released. The action also included the freezing of bank accounts, seizure of contraband, drastic limitation on travel, curfew and other severely restrictive measures. Some families learned several years later that their men were secretly shipped to internment camps around the country.

In March, 1942, when Bill was back home from college in Los Angeles, he learned that his old high school buddy, Johnny Kitsue and his entire family were detained in a Japanese internment camp outside of Bakersfield. A few weeks earlier,

Johnny had written Bill letters about the harsh life in the internment camps. Bill was shocked at this treatment of his Japanese friend, and vowed to do something about it. One night, he drove out in the middle of the night to the internment camp, armed with a flashlight, a shovel, and a care package for Johnny Kitsue and his family. Bill wasn't thinking clearly about how he was going to bust Johnny and his family out of prison, but he started to dig under the barbed wire fence with his shovel under cover of darkness in the cold night air. Fortunately for Bill, two Army Military Police drove up in their Jeep. After a cordial but firm conversation, the MPs concluded that the boy just missed his Japanese friend, so they let a sadder but wiser Bill go back home.

Bill learned that University of Arizona had a Horse Calvary at the U.S. Army Reserve Officer Training Corps building on campus. He was an expert horseman, caught and broke wild horses as a cowboy and participated in every rodeo event possible at the University of Arizona and Tucson rodeos. Of course, he wanted to defeat the Nazi and Japanese tyranny, but deep in the back of his mind, Bill knew the U.S. Army Reserve Officers' Training Corps played polo on weekends. That meant more time in the military for Bill on his beloved horses while serving his country, and getting paid for his service. In November, 1942, he joined the U. S. Horse Calvary.

Their mission was to teach the cadets how to ride the horses that would carry them into battle. The riding consisted of two-hour training sessions, twice a week with the mounted cadets. Instructors were Army sergeants and officers who were expert riders. Summer camp was a six-week training program where cadets rode every day and had overnight marches and learned combat tactics. Bill knew that the horses were remounts, a polite expression meaning somewhat less than top-quality animals. But he was good with horses and he knew their limits and what they were capable of. In addition to military training, cadets were required to participate in one of two activities – polo for the best horsemen and gymkhana, a jumping competition, for the less-skilled riders. With Bill's riding ability, they accepted him on the Polo team, University of Arizona, he noted, had one of the ten top cavalry training programs in the country, and its polo team was a national competitor.

Consequently, the U.S. Army Cavalry Division started liquidating their thousands of superbly bred and trained fighting horses, fearing that the Horse Calvary Division would be easily cut-down by Hitler's fearsome Panzer divisions.

Hitler's Panzer divisions made clear, by contrast, not by direct battle, the futility of the power of best-of breed Polish Cavalry. While it is a myth of propaganda that Hitler's Panzer division tanks mowed down the hapless Polish cavalry, it became clear to the U.S. Army that the Horse Cavalry Division would not win this war against German armored tanks. And while the Poles never used horses against German tanks, the mighty Soviet Army did, throwing their best cavalry officers against German armor, with terrifying results.

The U.S. Army eventually mechanized the Calvary using tanks, and horses ceased to exist.

Bill did what any normal American who wanted to fight the enemy would do, except he didn't consider much the consequences. He walked over to the U.S. Navy Recruiting Office and joined the United States Navy. He thought nothing about the fact that he was already in the U.S. Army Horse Cavalry Division.

America was at war on multiple fronts across the world. Bill wanted to serve his country and come back to finish his college degree.

It did not take many hours before Bill's U.S. Army Cavalry Corps Commanding Officer learned what he had done. Bill was brought in for a preliminary Army Court Martial Pretrial hearing for being technical Absent Without Leave.

Bill sat outside the military courthouse wondering what had he done wrong. He just wanted to serve his country, but how could he be an Army Horse Cavalry soldier without a horse? This young Irish-American teenager hung his head and prayed for wisdom. The military bailiff called his name to appear in front of the military judges.

Bill entered the military court, sharply saluting the judges. He was dressed in full U.S. Army Cavalry uniform, brass buttons polished, complete with his military-grade jodhpurs, with leather leg laces tightened to regulation tightness.

The charges were read out loud to him. They claimed he had abandoned his responsibilities as a United States Horse Cavalry Soldier. Bill studied the stern expressions of the Army judges. He prayed silently for wisdom and for God to give wings to his speech.

It was then that Bill saw his very own Commanding Officer was still wearing U.S. Army Horse Cavalry Jodhpurs and spurs. Why would anyone who had no horses anymore still wear the uniform of an Army horseman? Bill had his answer from above. He saluted the Army judges smartly, faced them squarely, and began to speak.

"Your Honors, I love the blue haze of the Arizona sunset in the desert lowlands. I love the camping in the high plains with my trusty Army horse I call Sunup. I love the sound of Jodhpur breeches slapping leather on horseflesh as our U.S. Army Cavalry thunders across the cactus-strewn alluvial plains. I love the sounds and the smells of our lathered Army horses snorting as they chomp on their well-deserved oats and hay. But how can any of this be possible without U.S. Army Cavalry horses? All that was taken away from us, from me. I cannot serve my country and win the war if I am just a rider without a horse. Your honors, even my U.S. Army saddle was taken away from me. I honestly thought I was fired from the Army. That's why I joined the United States Navy. That's why I ask your permission for transfer. Let me fight the enemy. Let us win. Let us do what President Teddy Roosevelt commanded us to do. He said, 'Do what you can, with what you have, where you are.'"

Bill saluted and stood at attention.

"You are dismissed while we deliberate," Bill's commanding officer said, visibly shaken but willing himself to frown.

Bill waited nervously outside. Less than five minutes had passed when his Commanding Officer opened the door, put his hand on Bill, and just looked at him.

"Your court martial has been dismissed," he said sharply. "As of February 6, 1943, you are honorably discharged. Go join your Navy men, fight the war, and come home safely."

Bill saluted and shook his Commanding Officer's hand.

The Officer leaned over to Bill and whispered, "When we win this war and you do come back, let's you and I go riding together, out in the blue haze of the Arizona sunset in the desert lowlands. By God, you got me with that one."

On his birthday, February 25, 1943, Bill was admitted officially into the Navy Reserve 11th Naval District for four years as member of V-1(G) Battalion. After training, he entered Southwest Louisiana Industrial Institute, in Lafayette, Louisiana into its V-12 and V-5 officer training programs. After passing Navy acceptance examination, Bill was shipped to Midshipman School at Northwestern University in Chicago as a commissioned ensign of the U.S. Navy Reserve. After having completed his officer training, he was shipped to

Coronado Island, California to begin training. Because of his natural athletic ability and his easy manner in water, he was assigned to the Underwater Demolition Team, or as the were called, The Frogmen.

In The Shedd, Bill doesn't tell me much about his Frogmen training. He murmured words like, "Hell Week," and "They had to separate the men from the boys." He said that "Many were called. Few were chosen." While we were sitting by the copper-top table, his son Justin asked his father, Bill, about his life as a Frogman.

"Bill," Justin said, "When I was a kid I saw a movie made in 1951 called "The Frogmen," with actor Richard Widmark, Dana Andrews, and Robert Wagner. They showed these men setting mines, disarming mines, cutting submarine fences, and gathering information about future attacks on the beach. The movie showed how the Frogmen were swiftly picked up by hooks from inflatable fast boats. If the Frogmen missed catching the hook, the movie made it look like the boat wouldn't pick them up. Was that what it was really like?"

Bill smiled and said, "Jus, you know how they do it in movies. It's all about the drama and action. No, the inflatable boats wouldn't just leave the Frogmen to drown or get eaten by sharks. But, if you missed catching the hook on the first go-around, I promise you the boat skipper would just sit back, smoke a Lucky Strike filter-less cigarette, and slowly mosey on back to pick your freezing butt up from the water. The Frogmen couldn't afford to be slow pokes."

The World War II news correspondent, Ernie Pyle, said of the Frogmen, "They're half fish and half nuts."

The Frogmen would be dropped off into perilous waters, set flotation mines, or destroy existing ones, cut submarine fences, take samples from the beach sand. In short, the Frogmen would to anything it takes to win the war and get out of the water they spent so much time in. They were the grandfathers of the U.S. Navy Seals, whose motto today still stands, "My Trident is a symbol of honor and heritage. Bestowed upon me by the heroes who have gone before, it embodies the trust of those I have sworn to protect.... I am never out of the fight..."

After training, Bill headed to the Pacific theater aboard the USS Grimes, a Haskell-class attack, 455-foot Navy ship, which was used to transport troops in and out of combat areas. The captain of the ship was J. McDonald Smith, and the ship was assigned to the Asiatic-Pacific Theater. Because of his leadership ability Bill quickly rose through ranks and became U.S. Navy Lieutenant, Junior Grade, and also Bat Group commander.

In August, 1944, the Allies liberated Paris, surviving the bloody beaches at Normandy. On October 20, 1944, General Douglas MacArthur, was forced in two years earlier to flee the Philippines with his troops and had famously said, "I shall return." He kept the promise and returned to the islands with an enormous invasion force and the largest assemblage of naval vessels in the history of mankind. For MacArthur, the liberation of the Philippines from the Japanese was the culmination of the war.

In November, Franklin Delano Roosevelt was elected for a fourth term as U.S. president. In Europe, Adolph Hitler was on the run back to his bunker in Berlin. The tide had turned against Japan, but they started kamikaze attacks on American ships, heavily damaging the aircraft carriers USS Lexington and USS Intrepid.

Prior to the attack on Iwo Jima, highly trained Frogmen swam ashore for reconnaissance and to collect beach soil samples. Once analyzed, the heavily volcanic soil samples indicated the assault forces would have some trouble getting off the beach.

By nightfall of the first day of the assault, February 19, 1945, thirty thousand Marines had landed, and more than five-hundred-fifty Marines were dead.

Marines who survived the conflict described the assault on the beaches as like "throwing human flesh against reinforced concrete."

The Battle of Iwo Jima was led by Admiral Nimitz, Commander in Chief for U.S. naval forces. Admiral Nimitz issued a directive to take the volcanic island. The battle, which Lt Gen Holland M Smith called the "most savage and costly battle in the history of the Marine Corps," pitted three Marine divisions against 21,000 Japanese defenders. The mission was to take the island so America and its allies could use the airfields as emergency landing bases for damaged airplanes returning from bombing raids on Japan. Also, by taking over the island, the American military would prevent the Japanese from using Iwo Jima as a base so their fighter planes could attack American B-29 bombers on their flights to Japan. Finally, Iwo Jima would have served as a stationing center for the eventual assault on Tokyo, but five months from the conflict at Iwo Jima, the two atom bombs would make that assault unnecessary.

The USS Grimes arrived fifteen days into the thirty-five-day Battle of Iwo Jima. Lieutenant William O'Brien was assigned to command a Landing Vehicle Tracked landing tank to take twenty Marines to shore. In the pitch black darkness, Bill ordered his five Navy crew members and the Marines onto the vehicle and waited for "Zero Hour." The Captain of the USS Grimes ordered every one to maintain absolute radio silence.

The previous day was one of the heaviest in the battle with over a hundred guns firing thousands of shells in just over an hour. Added to that, a battleship, a cruiser and three destroyers added hundreds of shells while Corsairs and Dauntless carried out ground attacks with bombs and napalm. The assault was staggered with the 5th Marine Division in the west to attack in the morning while the 4th Marine Division in the east was to launch their assault one hour later. Resistance was as strong as ever.

In the early morning light, the flotilla of dozens of Landing Vehicle Tracked moved slowly in formation far offshore, getting ready for "Zero Hour." Navy ships bombarded the island to clear a path off the beach. The landing LVTs had to idle for three hours in the sea as the Marines all boarded on. Nausea was beginning to spread. Nobody spoke much, and the radio crackled slightly. Ninety minutes to go.

Incredibly, a quiet but firm voice of the captain of the USS Grimes voice came over Bill's radio, "Advance Zero Hour by one hour. Maintain radio silence."

The landing on Iwo Jima was terrifying to both the Navy crews and the Marines they transported ashore. The instant the fleet of hundreds of LVTs and amphibian tanks landed, seven Japanese battalions opened fire on them. Nobody could see any Japanese soldiers, they were all dug in pill boxes on the hills or hiding in the thousands of blast craters made by the American bombers to soften them up. Bill commandeered his LVT to shore and dropped down the heavy armor-plated ramp door on the crashing waves at the beach. The sun was already up, ready to light the day. Bill and his crew sprayed the beach with their 75mm Howitzer and Browning machine gun, hoping to hit anyone other than American soldiers. The Marines bailed out of the LVT with lightning speed, all except for one petrified solder, a kid, really. He was paralyzed with fear and froze in his boots at the ramp door.

"Hit the beach, Marine!" Bill yelled at the trembling teenager.

The Marine still did not move, so Bill had to encourage him out of the LVT and shouted, "Give 'em hell, Johnny and brag about it to me tonight at the chow hall." He prayed that his attempt at bravado would give the young Marine courage.

For ten days, Lt. O'Brien did his duty on Iwo Jima, as Commander of any workable amphibious tank. He transported Marines to battle, picked up the wounded, and delivered supplies to the beach on this strategically important but forgivingly merciless island. The Marines lost 6,891 men in the Battle of Iwo Jima. Out of the 22,000 Japanese soldiers on the island, only 212 were taken prisoners. Bill realized just how far the Japanese soldiers were willing to sacrifice to keep their land, even mostly flat and featureless volcanic island like Iwo Jima.

After thirty-six days of fighting hand to hand combat, bombing, and Navy shelling, the Marines captured Mount Suribachi, the highest point of the island and bastion of the Japanese defense. That was the site of the iconic photo and statue of the six Marines, including fellow Arizonan, a Pima Indian named Ira Hayes, raising the American flag.

Always with that smile.

SOUVENIRS AND THE JAPANESE SURRENDER

After the Battle of Iwo Jima was over, the USS Grimes lifted anchor, and headed out to the open sea. The only thing the battle-weary, mentally and physically exhausted men aboard the USS Grimes wanted was some Shore Leave, fitting reward for a mission accomplished. They were all excited when "Grumpy Grimes," as the ship's crew secretly referred to Captain Smith, called over the ship's intercom, "Now here this. All Hands on Deck."

Hundreds of Marines and Navy men joined on deck, their haggard faces brightening up with eager anticipation to hear where they would get to go for Shore Leave.

Captain Grimes was in his Navy whites, showing no trace of the harrowing combat, raised his hands and waved triumphantly to the cheering men who attempted to line up in an orderly fashion on the deck.

"Men," the Captain bellowed, "I just want to say that the United States of America, your family and friends and I are proud of what you did on that blasted volcanic rock back there these past weeks. You'll go back home and tell stories about this, maybe even write books about it. Thank you for your dedication, your sacrifice, and your professional behavior."

The captain paused, looked admiringly at the men and then westward toward the South Pacific. Was that a clue as to where they were going?

"And so I want to give you, because you really deserve it an Atta Boy! Yes, you men, all of you, sailors, Marines, officers, and crew, deserve an Atta Boy. Thank you." he declared enthusiastically, pumping his fists jubilantly up and down.

Captain J. McDonald Smith saluted the men, issued the order to dismiss, turned on his heels, and returned to the bridge.

The next thing you heard were random heavy objects being hurled into the ocean below. Men were swirling and stabbing their arms in the air. The sailors turned to each other and started shouting, questioning, demanding someone repeat what the captain said.

Bill O'Brien was agitated and confused—but only for a few seconds. Ever the optimistic Irish, he looked out over the ocean, felt the wind in his face, and smelled the warm salty sea air. Then he counted his blessings, just as his mother taught him.

Bill spoke out loud, in sudden realization of a truth, "I'm alive, unhurt, mentally tough, and physically fit. My family is alive. Plus I still have a job and get paid for it, and I get free room and board. I'm in good shape. I miss my fallen shipmates, but they lay down their lives for freedom. Life is good. Praise the Lord."

On April 12, only 17 days after the Americans defeated the Japanese at Iwo Jima, President Franklin Delano Roosevelt, after months of declining health, died a of cerebral hemorrhage at the Little White House in Warm Springs, Georgia, the rehabilitation center for the treatment of polio that he founded. Vice President Truman took over the government reins and became the next President of the United States.

Rising to the awesome responsibility of filling Franklin D. Roosevelt's shoes, Truman grew tremendously in office, which must have astonished his former Kansas constituents.

The Allies were preparing for Operation Downfall, a massive invasion of Japan in October, 1945. The entire Allied Pacific fleet were going to assemble off the coast of Japan.

In a major turning point of World War II, on July 16, 1945, the first successful detonation of a nuclear weapon occurred in the White Sands Proving Ground in New Mexico. Code-named "Trinity," it was part of the U.S. Army's The Manhattan Project, a top secret research project begun in 1939 to build a nuclear bomb to stop the war.

As Vice President, in office for only six months, Truman did not know about The Manhattan Project. The top secret project was a complete surprise to him and President Roosevelt, whom Truman rarely saw, chose not to tell him. After the success of the Trinity test at White Sands, Truman gave the fateful executive order to drop a uranium atomic bomb on the Japanese city of Hiroshima. Then a few weeks later, Truman decided to drop a second bomb, a plutonium bomb on the city of Nagasaki. To this day, historians endlessly speculate why a second bomb was dropped. Whatever the reasons, President Truman took responsibility like a leader must, and he made a decision.

The entire Pacific fleet was underway north preparing to attack Tokyo under Admiral Halsey, and hundreds of thousands of lives were at risk on both sides of the fighting. Then, two atomic bombs were dropped over Japan at Hiroshima and Nagasaki on August 6 and 9, 1945, respectively, and Japan surrendered.

Four months earlier, Germany had surrendered after Hitler committed suicide.

After the surrender of the Empire of Japan was announced on August 15, 1945 the U.S.S. Grimes entered Tokyo Bay. Bill O'Brien was part of the Underwater Demolition Team, the first shipborne forces to set foot in Japan. Their mission was to check the beaches at Yokosuka, at the mouth of Tokyo Bay, and ensure that fortifications and ordnance were neutralized. There was also the very real threat of drifting mines that were still in the harbor.

On September 2, 1945, Japan's formal surrender took place aboard the U.S.S. Missouri, anchored in Tokyo Bay. The war was finally over. Bill still remembers the incredible sight of hundreds of thousands of white flags, all inserted neatly into Japanese naval ship cannons, land-based cannons, rifles, or being waved by Japanese soldiers on the shore. That scene became embedded into Bill's mind to this day as living proof of the power of healing, forgiveness, and reconciliation. Bill spoke of that day always with great reverence.

Bill was the leader of the First Division, and their assignment was to clear every Japanese away from the shore at the yacht harbor of Tokyo. After the clean-out, Bill and his boatswain mate decided to take a souvenir back to their ship. The souvenir was an abandoned thirty-two-foot Japanese teakwood speedboat floating outside the harbor. Bill's idea about the powerboat was for the Captain and his First Division to have a private shore transportation. To tow the speedboat up to the second deck of the Grimes, they put straps under the craft and the boomer had it hoisted onto the side of the ship. The speedboat was half way up when a booming voice came over the ship's intercom.

"O'Brien, to the bridge, on the double."

The voice was from the Executive Officer, the second in command of the ship who reports to the Commanding Officer. Bill walked, instead of jogged, up to the bridge. It was obvious the two men did not like each other.

"What do you think you are doing down there?" the officer asked brusquely.

He had a stern face and tried to appear tough.

"We're just bringing aboard a souvenir," Bill responded calmly, as if what he was doing was a natural thing.

"What do you mean a souvenir? What you're doing is looting. If you were caught looting you could be court-martialed. Put it back, O'Brien."

While on the bridge, Bill looked down to his boatswain mate standing by the starboard quarter and gave him the thumbs down signal and a half smile. Bill then joined his mate and the souvenir was dropped down into the water and set adrift in the harbor. It seemed like such a waste of a perfectly good teakwood speedboat.

During wartime, soldiers frequently brought home mementos as keepsakes to remind them of an important time of their lives. In fact, Bill came home with a centuries-old Samurai sword and a beautiful pair of U.S. Military binoculars that he had taken off a dead Japanese officer on the beach at Iwo Jima. The binoculars were from a fallen Marine, so Bill knew the dead Japanese soldier undoubtedly swiped it from him.

Bill kept the binoculars in honor of the fallen Marine. As for the Samurai sword, Bill eventually hung it on the wall of his den in Paradise Valley for forty-five years until he could figure out what to do with it. Finally, at his home, Bill gave the Samurai sword to his great Japanese friend, Hiroshi Watanabe, who had lost his father in that same war, to honor their friendship.

"I've already forgiven the Japanese for attacking us. It's time you take this sword back to Japan where it belongs," Bill said to Hiroshi as he handed him his treasured relic. Years later, Hiroshi Watanabe, a Japanese entrepreneur, named his new line of Jojoba oil-based Shampoos, "O'Brien's Shampoo." Jojoba oil is an oil extracted from the waxy seeds of a desert shrub, widely used in cosmetics. In the 1980s, Bill would be instrumental in developing Jojoba as an agricultural in Arizona. He would go on to found the International Jojoba Growers Association and traveled to Israel and Japan to give lectures on the plant.

After the two atom bombs were dropped on Japan, one of the missions of the USS Grimes was to bring food, blankets and medical supplies to the poor souls in Hiroshima and Nagasaki. After unloading the humanitarian supplies at Nagasaki, Bill decided he wanted to see for himself what an atom bomb could do. Since an atomic bomb had never been dropped outside the United States, nobody knew the lingering effects of nuclear radiation. Traveling with a platoon of Navy sailors and Marines, Bill sailed up the mouth of the Urakami River from Nagasaki. He and Navy Ensign, Joe Jertberg, walked through the entire bombed area. The extent of the vast blast site was evidence of the incredible destructive power of the atomic bomb. The scenery was surreal. Shrouded in the morning fog, Bill saw the charred remains of dogs, horses, and people. Three to four inches of dull gray ash covered the ground. As he approached near Ground Zero, he saw the roofs of houses scattered all over on the ground. Surprisingly, the walls, were blown inwards instead of outwards. Bill carefully side-stepped to avoid the separated head of a body, which looked like it would collapse like a large cigarette ash. Soon, towards the end of his tragic tour of the bombed out city, he saw there was nothing but the remains of a house covered with ash and burned trees ashes. All that was left standing in the house was a fractured toilet, a broken sink, and scattered household gadgets, harsh reminders that once there were people, and animals, and greenery.

For decades after Hiroshima and Nagasaki, Bill received letters each year from the US Navy, inquiring discreetly how he was doing. But as Bill told me, "What they really wanted to know each year was, since I walked through downtown Nagasaki a week after we dropped the bomb, am I still alive."

The USS Grimes continued their mission of mercy, unloading medical supplies, food, blankets and clothing to the survivors of Hiroshima and Nagasaki, Japan medicine, blankets and food. They sailed to The Philippines to restock for emergency supplies. So Bill saw, first hand, before the scientists, technicians, and military personnel ever began their hundreds of atomic tests, the chilling power of the atom vs. a human being.

THE PANAMA CANAL

After completing post-war duties, Bill was assigned as a quarterdeck officer on the USS Meriwether, another Haskell attack transport like the USS Grimes. The ship was part of Operation Magic Carpet, and the mission goal was to bring back more than eight million American soldiers from the European, Pacific, and Asian theaters.

The ship was heading home to Boston, Massachusetts, for decommissioning at the Virginia Navy Yard. Captain Angus Meade Cohan, who commanded the ship was a graduate of the U.S. Naval Academy in Annapolis and he was a boxer like Bill. The two officers loved to box each other, both for the love of the sport and to keep in shape on the voyage back home. The two became good friends and had a mutual respect for their boxing skills.

Looking at the naval maps and studying the sea route to Boston, Bill seized on a great opportunity. He suggested to the Captain to stop at the nearest port to repair the damaged forward quarter of the ship. This would reduce the risk of leakage from the hull and the idea would avoid the extra dock time at the overbooked Virgina Navy Yard to wait for repairs. The captain liked Bill's idea. After discussing the plan with his superiors, the Captain of the USS Meriwether changed course to Bill's recommendation, the closest shipyard, the resort town of Acapulco, Mexico.

Bill's first view, sailing in to Acapulco, was the deep semi-circular bay where shipping and cruise lines run between Panama and California. It still is Mexico's largest beach and most well-known beach resort. Acapulco was famous for its nightlife and a getaway for Hollywood stars and millionaires. It was the perfect place for the Meriwether crew to spend a couple of weeks while waiting for the repairs.

After the short stay in Acapulco, they sailed down the west coast of the Latin America to the Panama Canal. Bill was full of excitement. He had won a search-and-rescue competition that was among the deck officers. They tried to maneuver the seventeen-ton vessel around an orange life preserver and approach it as if there was a man-overboard. The winner's prize was to be the Officer of the Deck going through the Panama Canal. A flotilla of cargo ships waited their scheduled turn to enter the canal for the ten hour sail across to the city of Colon. In order to see the real beauty of nature going through the lakes and narrow passages, first the vessel had to go through the set of locks. Bill watched in amazement as the vessel entered the first chamber and the heavy gate closed behind it. The vessel was then lifted to over ninety-feet above sea level by water transported into the locked chamber. Finally, the locomotives that ride on rails alongside the lock tied up the vessel to help it move steadily to the next lock.

Bill felt honored, as well as thrilled, to be on the bridge to see and appreciate first hand the enormity and engineering of that great American endeavor and to say a prayer for the number of American lives that it cost.

The narrow dreamlike passing, especially the first part of the journey, was an amazing experience. He never forgot how incredible it was to see the vessel, at times, nearly scraping the land and beautiful trees which were ladened with deep green leaves and used as a home for colorful birds. The trees were so close one almost could touch them.

"Thank goodness the responsibility of guiding the ship through the canal belonged to a professional pilot, he is incredible," Bill whispered with admiration.

After Bill turned over the ship to Captain Cohan with a reluctant smile. They sailed from Colon, Panama to the Naval Yard in Virginia.

Knowing that his navy days were coming to an end and that his restless spirit wasn't use to staying idle, Bill looked into enrolling in to the University of Arizona. Unfortunately he was told that, because of the large number of returning veterans, it would be well over a year and a half before he could enroll back in college.

Turning to me in The Shedd, Bill said, in sudden realization of a truth, "You know, except for the shooting, I had a terrific time during the war."

THANKSGIVING DAY BOXING MATCH

Shortly after docking in to the Naval Yard in Virginia, Bill was given three days of Shore Leave for Thanksgiving. He arrived at his parents house on the same day as his younger brother Don, who was also on a Shore Leave. Don was drafted into the U.S. Navy that July, two months before Japan surrendered. Father and Mother were proud to see their young men dressed in their full military uniforms and happy that they were safe.

Everybody hugged each other.

"Your brother Jim's not here yet, said Mother. "Just look at you. You boys have all grown up."

They went inside to the living room to catch up on life. Several minutes later, there was a knock on the door.

"Ah, that would be Jim," Mother said, and got up to answer the door.

Several minutes later, a visibly shaken Mother slowly came back to the living room. She carrying with a heavy package bearing an official U.S. Army return address. Her face was pale and she looked at her family with tears in her eyes.

During the war, families all across the country received packages like this. It usually meant their sons were dead, and the contents were the personal effects. Pretty soon the families could expect a knock on the door and receive the news from grim-faced military men of their sons' demise.

Bill opened the package, shielding its contents from his parents so he could see it first. What he saw filled him with dread. It was the worst sight he could imagine. It was brother Jim's U.S. Army Sargent's helmet. Just then, Bill noticed the helmet was pierced through with bullet holes, and his heart started beating faster. Bill quickly put the helmet on and then then inserted a knitting needle through a bullet hole on one side and out a hole on the other side. The knitting needle skimmed the top of Bill's head, so the O'Brien family all thought that Jim was surely dead. In the package, not even the sight of Jim's Silver Star for bravery, Purple Heart, Bronze Stars, and many combat war ribbons, bronze medallions, and multi-colored stripes could console the quietly trembling family.

Suddenly, there was a pounding at the front door.

"This was it," Bill told us in The Shedd, "Here come the U.S. Army officers with their all-too-common speech, 'We regret to inform you that your son James Murray O'Brien is dead. He died on the field of battle in service to this country.'"

Since Bill was the oldest, he went to open the door, steeling his mind and hardening his heart for the bad news to come.

He almost feinted right there himself. It was brother Jim back from the war!

"Hiya, Bill," Jim shouted, giving him a bear hug and slugging Bill's right shoulder. Jim put his right arm around Bill's neck and they clumsily danced in wild circles, banging against the hallway walls.

"Jim's alive!" Bill thought, as he slid his body along down the hallway, trying to regain stability. "He made it!"

After a while of crying, laughing, and hugging, the family sat down to enjoy their Thanksgiving dinner Mother had prepared. They reminisced how all three of their sons had to take boxing lessons from age eight on from those old Mexican ex-boxing champs. They were fairly equally matched in speed, precision, agility, and style. Brother Jim was California Amateur State Champion and also boxed in the Army. Bill was Collegiate Champion in the featherweight class. Without false modesty, Bill said, he was pretty good, but Don was better." Don was Golden Gloves champion west of the Mississippi, and he placed second in the Pacific West Coast Intercollegiate Competition. When Bill asked Don why he didn't take first place in the Pacific West Coast Intercollegiate Competition, Don said, with his classic grace and humility, "There I met my match."

Father and Mother were thrilled to have their three boys at home back from the war. Their daughter, Jane, was back east helping in the war effort with her husband, Justin Dart, and their fifth anniversary was coming up the next month. All three boys had grown up. Jim developed massive a chest and shoulders, Bill looked quick and wiry, and Don, fresh out of high school, was getting used to Navy life, and he looked tough.

It was an emotional evening, seeing their three war hero sons at the dinner table, safe and sound, all talking at once at the dinner table. What a life they've all had, but through it all, the O'Briens were a family. They had each other, and that was true wealth. After a while, Don got up and said to Bill and Jim he was going out to see some of his buddies and he would see them later.

War or no war, Mother ran a tight ship in the home, and rules were rules. It was Jim and Bill's turn to do the dishes, and there were plenty piled up that Thanksgiving night.

"You wash. I'll dry," Jim said crisply in what Bill thought was an authoritative tone of voice.

Bill was always very tuned in to people's tone of voice, and that ability had served him well. He knew that a person's tone of voice was one of the clues to their personality, mood, and behavior.

Jim started washing his hands. Bill sorted the dishes. He thought Jim was sure taking his sweet time with that soap. Two minutes was too long.

Bill started to get irritated.

"Say, um, Billy…" Jim said in a cheerful voice, avoiding Bill's eyes.

That was a cheap shot, and Jim knew it. Bill always hated to be called, "Billy." A storm was brewing in their minds.

"…Isn't the name of your Navy tugboat the USS Grimey?" Jim said in a mocking tone, really emphasizing the last word.

"It's not a tugboat, Jimmy." Bill shot back. His blood was starting to boil. "It's a Haskell-class attack transport."

There was dead silence for what seemed to Bill like an eternity. Jim finally turned off the water and began drying his hands.

As they did the dishes in the thick silence, the air in the kitchen was heavy with memories of past grievances that remained unspoken. Maybe it was the horrors of the war and the bloodshed they had experienced that turned their minds inward.

Beginning to get steaming mad, but without really knowing why, Bill started to angrily wash plates, glasses, and silverware. He gradually became more and more aggressive in his kitchen duties, clattering plates and clanging silverware. Jim dried the dinnerware while avoiding eye contact.

Now really angry, Bill was itching for a fight. He wanted to find out just how much the war had turned these two boys into men.

Seizing the moment, and, just for fun, Jim commanded, "Get me a dry towel!"

Without even looking at his brother, Jim threw the wet towel in Bill's direction. He knew this night had to come to a head. Jim loved his brother, but he wanted Bill to settle down and grow up.

Bill decided to completely ignore his brother.

"I told you to get a dry towel," Jim repeated in an authoritative voice, while struggling to suppress a smile. It was all an act, just roughhousing like when they were kids. But Bill saw things differently.

"I've been waiting for this moment," Bill said as he raised his fists and they squared off, right in the O'Brien family kitchen.

"Come on Billy. You don't want to do this." Jim said, with a half-smile and eyebrows raised in mock fear.

Bill would not listen. He raised his fists, up to eye-level, and he glared at his big brother.

He felt Jim's fist come out of nowhere. How could he be that fast? He never saw it coming. Then darkness. Then nothing, nothing at all.

The next thing Bill saw was the white plaster kitchen ceiling. It was slowly spiraling somehow. There were those gray globby spheres again, spinning in circles over his head, not at all like the ones you see in the funny books, as Bill had told it before.

He blinked his eyes, and rubbed his jaw and slowly raised up off the kitchen floor.

From that day on, Jim was Bill's hero.

Bill handed him another dry towel and said, "I never saw it coming, Jim but I gotta know. Was it a left or a right?

"Billy boy, said Jim, helping his brother up from the linoleum floor, "It was the Hammer of Thor from the skies above. So next time, look up, brother."

ARUBA

After Bill had tried to re-enroll at University of Arizona he was told that it would be well over two years before he could return as a junior in college.

Never one to let an obstacle slow him down, a few day after he returned to the Naval Yard in Virginia, he took a taxi to the Pentagon in Arlington, Virginia. Wearing his full-dress white U.S. Naval Officer's uniform, he flagged down a Seaman First Class on roller skating in the hall right past him.

"Why are you on kiddy skates?" Bill asked, staring at the man's laced up boots on wheels.

"We have miles of hallways inside the Pentagon," the Seaman proudly declared. My skates, Sir, save me time and helps in some small way with the war effort because the brass has faster access to information."

Bill asked the Seaman to tell him where the Admiral was. The young Navy man skated Bill to the right place. The door was open.

"Good day, Admiral," said Bill, who saluted and put his officer's cap under his left arm. "My name is Bill O'Brien, Lieutenant, Jr. Grade of the United States Navy, just back from the Asiatic/Pacific Theater. I would like to re-up for about six months because I cannot get back into my college program until August. I'm fluent in Spanish, because I grew up with Mexican kids in elementary and high school. I know how to get along with them because I'm Irish. And Mexicans and Irish are similar in so many ways. I'm ready to serve anywhere in Latin America or South America. And I'm ready to leave tonight. I respectfully request to re-up, Sir!"

"Thank you for your service to America," the Admiral said.

He opened a massive book, turned the pages, and said, "Let me see what's available."

The admiral looked up from his big Pentagon personnel book, he thought for a moment, then allowed a faint smile on his face and said. "Young man, how would you like to become the U.S. Navy Commanding Officer of Aruba in the Dutch West Indies.

Bill did not hesitate for a second. "Fine, sir, when I am going. Tonight?"

"As soon as we get your papers ready. Shouldn't take but a day," the Admiral responded as he waved at Bill and picked up the phone, pretending to be otherwise occupied.

On his way out. Bill leaned over and whispered to the Admiral's secretary "Where in the world is Aruba and what are we doing there?"

The Admiral's secretary looked at the young Lieutenant officer and gave him a short history lesson about the island. "Aruba is twenty miles northeast of Venezuela. In 1636, Aruba was acquired by the Netherlands and remained under their control for nearly two centuries. Standard Oil Refinery of New Jersey runs the Lago oil refinery there, the largest in the Western Hemisphere. Dutch-owned Shell Oil Refinery own the other major refinery and both have been extremely important during the war for aviation fuel. Three years earlier the Germans tried to attack one of the refineries but ultimately were chased away. Because the Shell refinery had been attacked by Hitler's Navy, America offered to protect both refineries oil supplies until the end of the War. The island is already in the process of trying to gain independence from the Dutch. The current U.S. Naval Commander of Aruba has had enough of this post and this war. He is over seventy-years-old, and he wants to come back home. Don't expect a lot of love from him. He's probably half a century older than you. Good luck with that."

Bill looked at the secretary and said, "I'm impressed! How do you know all that about such a little island?"

"Because it's my business to know everything. Good day, sir." She went back doing her work.

Bill politely thanked the secretary for her helpful report and left the office. He found his way through the endless Pentagon corridors into the light of day. As he left the Pentagon, Bill suddenly realized that he fully understood the difference between a government bureaucrat and a business executive.

Bill arrived in the Caribbean island of Aruba several weeks later. The military Jeep dropped him off at the gate and he then greeted the current Commanding Officer of Aruba.

The older man's look of disdain could barely be disguised, as if to say, "I'm being replaced by this, a man child?"

But he gave Bill the file and left without looking back. Bill watched the older man as the Jeep carried him out of the base. Now that the war was over most men were headed home, wherever that may be.

Bill O'Brien's new Navy job sounded impressive to his family and friends but he wasn't really impressed himself. According to him, he was just stalling for time until he could go back to University of Arizona. For the American government O'Brien was the Naval Base Commanding Officer of Aruba, but because the base was eventually closing, hundreds of military men stationed in the island went home. They were replaced with three new military officers and eighteen Navy Seamen, a crew that was given four military station wagons and a Navy aircraft, with a mechanic, who was also the pilot.

There were still tremendous responsibilities, therefore Bill O'Brien, now twenty-three-years-old was also the Port Director, Routing Officer, and Communications Officer.

The international refinery companies provided work for about a quarter of the island's residents.

Bill took a liking to the Caribbean Steel Drum music and was amazed to learn that it was an American-influenced invention. During the war the U.S. Navy had to provide fuel for the millions of machines and military equipment. The forty-two-gallon steel cans full of gasoline and oil just tossed over the railing, and they floated to wherever they found land. When so many steel drums started arriving on the shores of the Caribbean islands, the local residents discovered that the cans made a delightful thumping sound. Because of the waves and turbulent waters, the cans got banged up, and the pitch and tone of the lids of each steel drum was somewhat different, and each made different sounds. The natives started fashioning out new musical instruments from these disposable objects.

Bill had been on training missions in many places, but Aruba's warm, turquoise-colored, crystal clear salt water was the best he had seen. The marine life was incredible and it was a great place to dive and explore.

Aruba was full of fascinating animal and plant life, some of which are found nowhere else but on this island. For instance, the Divi Divi tree, which is permanently bent at a nearly right angle and its Medusa-like branches jut out, seemingly swept back by the wind. Bill felt a touch of Arizona when he gazed from his Navy Jeep at the widespread Pines, Hibiscus, Wild Orchids, many cacti, and the pink and magenta Bougainvillea bushes. It was in Aruba that Bill discovered that the Agave plant, known as the Aloe Vera plant was grown commercially and shipped to many destinations.

For the small base the workload was enormous. Bill was responsible for the arrival and departure times of tankers. He had to get the berthed ones loaded with oil and back on their way before the empty ships arrived. It took concentration and coordination with Standard Oil, Royal Dutch Shell, the Navy, and even the State Department.

Another of Bill's responsibilities was to map and track the position of floating German mines, released by the thousands by German submarines during the war. Dredging for mines and throwing nets were effective strategies to capture these mines that were still floating pointlessly across the world.

This Caribbean island had important oil refineries which provided fuel to Allied ships and submarines during the war. Aruba was a top target for flotation mines released by the Germans. Since Bill was strong in math and deep-water ocean navigation, he was able to track the paths of these active deadly messengers. In the days before computers, calculators, or the Internet, Bill and the rest of the crew had to rely only on their Navy-issued, wooden slide rule, to track and stop these mines. They had to account for many variables, Gulf Stream currents, wind speed, water temperature, and climate. It was tedious, boring, and absolutely essential. Frequently, Bill would be jolted awake in the middle of the night, rush down to his Naval office to consult his nautical maps, make some quick calculations, and then make a call to U.S. Naval Command at Guantanamo Bay to alert the Navy of the location of the mines. These floating mine dreams helped Bill understand the power of his subconscious mind. From then on, Bill would use the creative energy of his sleeping mind to solve problems, look for opportunities, and create new ideas that would benefit himself, his family, and his business.

Venezuela, was about an hour's boat ride from the coast of Aruba. The high plateau country of Venezuela was famous for their cattle ranches, and cattle prices were cheap there. Bill learned this from the Dutch banker on Aruba who handled oil transactions between the U.S. Government and the oil companies who operated their refineries on the island. With his earlier experience in Arizona on cattle ranches, Bill's business mind was as usual on high alert. For shore leave, once he went to the Venezuelan high plateau and he met with local cattle ranchers about how to lease or purchase a cattle ranch. Bill mulled over the idea of running his own cattle ranch in Venezuela, but he felt Arizona was his true home. Bill O'Brien who has always been interested in history, and he read the detailed account history of the U.S. Naval base on Aruba. He read the official contract signed by the United States and the Netherlands called the "Lend Lease Agreement," to protect the two island refineries during World War II. After doing some calculations, Bill estimated that, according to the contract, the Dutch government owed the United States Government thirteen-million dollars as their share of the cost for the refinery and protection during the war. The loan was to be immediately paid in full, provided the United States and its European allies defeated Hitler and the Axis powers.

Bill contacted the United States Naval Command at Guantanamo Bay, Cuba and asked how to collect the money owed to United States Government.

"Collecting the money is not our jurisdiction, it's is the State Department's job." said the man on the other line with an irritated voice.

"Obviously a bureaucrat who doesn't care about taxpayer money," Bill thought.

He then contacted the State Department, and, after being bounced around from one person to another, he finally found someone to answer his question, but their response was apathetic and uncaring.

Due to the lack of interest on collecting a legitimate debt from a European country, Bill decided to take action for himself. He typed up an invoice for $13,000,000 on Navy stationery, drove his Jeep over to Oranjestad, Aruba's capital and largest city at the east end of the island. He entered the Dutch government administration building and asked to see whomever was in charge. A distinguished looking man came out fairly quickly and asked how he could help. Bill introduced himself, explained the nature of his visit, presented the invoice on behalf of the United States of America, and said goodbye to the representative of the Dutch government.

Driving back to the Navy base, Bill felt pleased and proud for what he had done.

The act generated some action but not the way Bill was hoping for.

Two suited man from the State Department arrived about a week later.

"Where the hell did you get the authority to act on the State Department's behalf," one of the men who seemed in charge barked at Bill.

"First of all I don't know who you are" Bill responded, "I need to check with Washington."

The two men seemed annoyed but that did not bother Bill.

After receiving a confirmation from Washington as to who they were, Bill responded calmly, "Well, let me show you."

He showed them his calculations and a copy of the signed "Lend Lease Agreement" where it was all spelled out. The men wanted the documents and Bill gave them to them after requiring a signed receipt. The money owed to the American Government was from the already sold Navy equipment, land and buildings to the Dutch island government. The State Department assumed the job of collecting the money. It was interesting that there was very little knowledge on how to collect, and Bill wasn't very impressed at the business acumen of the American government.

The two State Department representatives turned and left, only saying goodbye over their shoulder to Bill. "I will never work for the government," Bill said out loud, shaking his headMonths later, after the Aruba base was turned back over to the Netherlands government, Bill stopped at Guantanamo to pay respects to the Commanding Officer who had read all about the money ordeal and belly-laughed at the incident.

"I will get the government moving on this matter O'Brien," the admiral affirmed.

"Thank you, sir," and Bill was on his way back. The only souvenir he brought from Aruba was a case of scotch for his folks. Having served his country, Bill was honorably discharged from the Navy. Brother Jim had returned to Los Angeles a year earlier, after serving as a highly decorated sergeant in the U.S. Army in the Pacific. Don finished his Navy service after a year and enrolled at UCLA to get his business degree. When Bill came home, Don and Jim came over to their parent's house for a welcome home. Amazingly, nothing seemed changed. Mother and Father looked great. They were still in the Perkins Street house north of Sunset Boulevard in Brentwood. During the dinner conversation between the three brothers about their military adventures, the excitement of returning home and the physical and emotional roller coaster of war, Bill realized that these were life changing moments. He had to re-adjust to peacetime and use these moments of change to be prepare for his future.

That evening, he knew what he was going to do. First he was going to go back to finish college at University of Arizona in Tucson as soon as a space opened up. On August 6, 1946, Bill re-enrolled as a junior at University of Arizona.

Some months later, Bill's sister Jane and Justin Dart had moved from Medfield, Massachusetts to Los Angeles, which was great for the O'Brien family. Jane loved New England, but Justin was building the biggest drug store in the world in Los Angeles at Beverly and La Cienega. That was near where Bill used to work as a carryout boy at the Farmer's Market. Brother Jim met many Irish folks while in the military and he knew almost every Irish song ever written. When Jim got back from the Army, he had gotten a job at a top radio station in Hollywood, and after work he often met with his Irish friends in a singing Irish pub. Don was in college and doing great.

BACK AT UNIVERSITY OF ARIZONA

After waiting more than two years, in August, 1946, Bill could finally restart his college program at University of Arizona, finish that college degree and get on with his life.

College life was different from what he remembered. The students were younger and they didn't seem very mature. He found himself gravitating toward students who had served in the war because they had similar experiences. For example, as a freshman, he had become friends and boxed with Bill Ritchie who was respected by all of his classmates. Ritchie later became a great Arizona heavyweight boxing champion who later became a judge.

After the Saturday night games, Bill and his classmates would head down to the border of Nogales and, once across the border they would hit the cantinas to dance to the Mariachi bands. They usually left the border late at night to drive for the ninety-minute trip back, driving on what is still called, Calle de Muerte. It is a wonder that they all survived that dangerous highway over their many trips.

A year after his return to college, Bill tried his hand in politics when he decided to run against Morris "Mo" Udall for University of Arizona Student President. Bill used all his innovative leadership skills to run. He and his campaign manager, James McNulty, even held midnight torchlight parades through the U of A fraternity and sorority houses. It helped that most students knew Bill because he was a very vigorous Yell Leader at all the U of A football games. After a tight race, Mo Udall won the election. Bill did not like to lose, so he knew politics would not be the career for him. After the election was over, Mo Udall approached Bill.

"I'd like to appoint you to be Chairman of the University of Arizona Traditions Committee," Mo Udall said to Bill.

This was a big deal. It meant coordinating all the service clubs, the Yell Leaders, some fraternity events, senior proms, Freshman Day and major U of A traditions. Best of all, it meant Bill would run the Coca Cola franchise with his former campaign manager, James McNulty, at all of the football games. That was a business opportunity that was worth thousands of dollars per month.

"Mo, why would you select me?" asked Bill, with a look of puzzlement on his face. "I was, after all, your opponent. We were at each other tooth and nail."

Mo smiled, as good politicians always do, and said, "Bill, I like you. You're a Good Hoss."

Bill shook Mo's hand and thanked him.

"This guy is good, and he'll go far—he is a real politician," Bill thought.

Indeed, Morris, "Mo" Udall went on to become a professional basketball player with the Denver Nuggets during their National Basketball League period. He later became Arizona's United States Congressman. In 1976, Mo Udall ran for the Democratic primary nomination for President, coming in second place to Jimmy Carter.

Bill was always very active on campus, and thanks in part to his military service, he was a natural leader. As a freshman, he had joined the fraternity, Phi Gamma Delta and he was voted Treasurer. His first order of business was to examine why the fraternity's kitchen budget was so high. He discovered that the fifty or so fraternity members were having Top Sirloin, Porterhouse, and T-bone steaks almost every single night. In addition, the cook was buying the steaks in single packets each at the local grocery stores. Since Bill knew how to field dress wild game while hunting in Arizona, he started ordering whole sides of beef from a Tucson meat processing plant and taught the cook how to cut it up as needed for each meal. That saved Phi Gamma Delta thousands of dollars per year on food. That experience taught him the importance of cash flow and cutting costs.

He was one of the Yell Leaders on the University of Arizona football team, at a time when women were starting to be included on the field as cheerleaders.

University of Arizona was one of the first school in the nation to hold intercollegiate rodeos. Bill entered almost every event and won lots of ribbons, applause, and the admiration of spectators and, more importantly, of his peers.

"Blue ribbon in the rodeo is first place of course," Bill told us in The Shedd.

"Then of course, red for second place, then yellow, white, pink, green, purple, and brown for eighth place. But, even if you get bucked off, or get a Brownie for eighth place, what's really important is that you're in the arena. You're participating, you're engaged, whether in an event or in life.

As University of Arizona Traditions Chairman, Bill had to know the many college traditions of the university, annual events, and the school's history as a land grant college founded sixty years earlier. He even had to monitor the practice he disliked called hazing, an ancient practice of rituals and other activities involving harassment, abuse or humiliation used as a way of initiating a person into a group. A natural public relations man with an ability to craft a story the reporters wanted, Bill was mentioned for his college activities in dozens of stories in the local newspapers.

In 1947, Bill was finally a senior at University of Arizona. On the world's stage, Harry S Truman was President. Truman expanded Roosevelt's large social programs including social security and the G.I. Bill. The G.I bill allowed war veterans to go to college.

The world kept on turning, even as Bill was eager to graduate and get out in the arena of life. He thought that, actually, being away from college during the war had a positive influence on his Grade Point Average. He was now more mature and he was taking classes that he really enjoyed, like Agriculture, Economics, Business Management, and Marketing.

MEETING SADA

Bill was twenty-four-years old when he came home May, 1947, to Los Angeles on summer break from his senior year at University of Arizona He was staying at his parent's house on Perkins Street. His parents were thrilled to listen as Bill regaled them with his exciting stories of college life and his war stories. They were so proud that Bill had found his footing. Jim and Don had jobs. America was moving again, having shaken off the Great Depression doldrums, or maybe the American people were just fed up with being depressed.

Bill had just received a letter from University of Arizona that said the school would accept his four units of economic and marketing credits earned as midshipman at Northwestern University, as well as three units from Southwestern Louisiana Institute where he was the Navy unit butcher. That meant that he had earned enough units to graduate at mid-term in May 26, 1948, earlier than he had planned. Bill could graduate with what would now be called an Agri-business degree, because he majored in Agriculture with a minor in international finance.

It was good to be home, Bill thought, knowing that home was wherever his family was. Two years earlier Bill's sister Jane and Justin Dart, now head of United Rexall Drugstores, had moved the company headquarters from Boston to Los Angeles. It was good to have everyone in the same town again. While back home, Jane invited Bill to come over for dinner to meet Stephen and Priscilla Paine and their daughter, Sarah. In Boston, the Paines and the Darts were next-door-neighbors and had become great friends. Sarah and her parents had come from Boston to attend the wedding of Sarah's brother.

When Bill O'Brien and Sarah Paine first met at the Darts, it was love at first sight. During Sarah's short visit in Los Angeles that summer, she and Bill became inseparable. During that week, they would often miss family meals and just escape in Bill's ten-year-old 1937 banged up Studebaker pickup and dash over to Santa Monica Beach Club for a swim or to play tennis. Even strangers who saw the couple from a distance could tell that they were in love. But Bill had a problem. He lived in Los Angeles, and Sarah Paine lived across the country in Boston. Somebody had to move.

The day before the wedding of Sarah Paine's brother, in the living room of the O'Brien's house, Jane and her mother were talking excitedly about the wedding. Bill was in the kitchen making coffee. Then he overheard Jane and her mother talking about Sarah Paine. As he came out with the coffee on a tray Bill wasn't sure if they meant for him to hear their conversation. But, he realized his heart was pounding.

He finally knew in his heart, mind, and spirit, what he wanted to do.

"Hey, Sis," Bill interrupted, with an anxious voice. "Could I use your convertible?"

"Sure Bill, what's the occasion?" Jane asked.

"Oh, I just gotta do something important." Bill said trying to look composed.

Bill's mission was to see Steve Paine over at the Darts and ask him for Sarah's hand in marriage. While his decision seemed sudden, perhaps irrational, it was not uncommon. During World War II, romance continued to flourish. The dangers of war and the possibility of separation caused many young lovers to throw caution to the wind.

Bill knew that, to make an impression on Stephen Paine, his possible future father-in-law, he didn't want to drive up in his old 1937 Studebaker pick-up truck. He drove over the convertible and asked Mr. Paine if they could go for a ride up the coast toward Malibu.

As they drove toward the beach city, Bill and Steve talked about everything that afternoon, the stars, the ocean, and the weather, everything, except what Bill wanted to ask. The older man had seen what was so obvious to everybody else who had seen the couple that week. Finally, Bill gathered up his courage.

"Mr. Paine, I want to ask you for something."

Long thoughtful silence.

"Call me Steve," Mr. Paine said, relieved that Bill finally got around to why they had been driving up and down the California coast for more than an hour. That broke the ice. Bill asked him for Shara's hand in marriage.

Steve Paine studied Bill's face for a moment. Bill was well-mannered, a charmer and he had military discipline. He saw that Bill could get along with everybody, especially Sarah. It was obvious that Sarah and Bill and Bill were in love. The only challenge Steve Paine thought would be if Bill decided to come back to Boston to work after he married Sarah.

After a brief silence, Steve Paine gave his consent. Bill's heart was filled with joy.

They turned around and drove back to the Dart's home. It was still early and the Paines and the Darts went swimming in the ocean at Santa Monica Beach Club.

When they returned to the Dart's home, Bill built a fire while Sada, as Sarah liked to be called, made hot chocolate, as the family milled around somewhat nervously. Everything was just right. Sada stood in front of the hot fire looking so beautiful. Bill walked up to her. Everyone was watching.

He got down on one knee and asked, "Sada, I love you with all my heart. I want to spend the rest of my life with you. I will make you happy. Will you marry me?"

Sada's entire face became a blissful smile, her eyes sparkled and she said "Yes, Bill, I will."

The positive spiritual and emotional energy was so powerful in the room. Everyone was laughing, crying, hugging, and shaking hands. Even the Dart's Golden Labrador Retriever came bounding into the living room and could hardly be restrained. Bill and Sada kissed and hugged again and had another hot chocolate. Bill drove home feeling more exhilarated than he had ever known was possible. The next day he took Sada to his parent's place on Perkins Street and told them the news. They were elated and everyone hugged.

Then he asked his dear Irish mother, to walk with them in the back yard.

"Mother, so now you know Sada and I have made a decision to get married for the rest of our lives, for better and for worse. Could you give us some advice that will help us in our marriage?" Bill asked, expecting deep and profound advice moral virtues, love or wisdom.

The three were walking arm in arm between the Avocado trees.

Mother stopped in her tracks, looked at Bill with those piercing eyes and said, "Bill, keep your stories short and snappy. And Sada, don't ever pass up a ladies restroom."

And that was that.

Even as Bill told me that story in The Shedd in his home in Paradise Valley, you could plainly see that he was still mystified about that incredibly practical life wisdom from his Irish mother.

Sada and Bill knew that their marriage had the blessings of everybody. They promised to love one another for the rest of their lives. Sada and her family said their goodbyes and went back to Boston with her parents. During the next year, while waiting for Bill to graduate, she volunteered as a medical aid in Boston caring for wounded war veterans. It was going to be a long year and she wanted to keep busy.

THE WEDDING AND THE IRISH

Bill had to drive back to Tucson to finish his final year at University of Arizona, so he would graduate, then they would get married. They set the date for a year later, June 16, 1948.

Bill hurled himself into his studies determined to finish college, eager to be with Sada.

A few years earlier, Bill's good friend Phyllis Draper would drive him to small rodeos where he would sign up for bronc riding or bull riding on Sundays. Phyllis introduced Bill to her dad, Paul Draper who was a Boston wool merchant. He had suggested that Bill should come to see him if he was ever in Boston.

Boston was the center of the wool business at that time. Bill decided to write his Economics thesis on the Boston wool market and became fascinated with this commodity. For his research, Bill got to know a lot of Arizona sheep farmers in Rimrock and Flagstaff and he attended plenty of sheep auctions to see how they moved the market.

When he officially finished his final exams, he was so anxious to see Sada, he didn't even bother to attend his University of Arizona graduation ceremony. He told them to mail his U of A diploma to his parents. He knew what he wanted to do with his life. Bill drove back to Los Angeles to see his parents. He then sold his Studebaker pick-up for one thousand dollars and used the money to buy a diamond ring for Sada. Now, cowboys love their pick-up trucks, but there was nothing more important than to give a beautiful diamond wedding ring to the love of his life. With the rest of the money from selling the Studebaker he bought an airplane ticket to Boston.

When Bill arrived in Boston, after reuniting with Sada and paid his respects, he headed straight to Mr. Paul Draper's office.

There he was greeted with a big smile.

Bill returned the smile, took a deep breath, and got right into the point, "Mr. Draper, I came here to ask you for work.

Mr. Draper responded, "Do you want work or do you want opportunity?" The question was a bit of a surprise for Bill.

"Opportunity of course," Bill answered.

"The Opportunity pays two-hundred-sixty dollars a week." Mr. Draper said jokingly. "You'll learn everything you want to know about the wool business from the ground up, and the opportunity to have a better life will come. If you agree, you'd start two weeks from now."

"I accept your opportunity. Thank you, Mr. Draper." Bill said, stepping forward and shaking Mr. Draper's hand.

"Call me Paul," Mr. Draper said as Bill was walking away.

Walking on air, Bill O'Brien had done it. He found the girl of his dreams, finished college, and he found an opportunity that eventually was going to change his and Sada's life.

Steve Paine offered Bill accommodations in a quest house on his farm.

Apple Knoll Farms, in Millis, Massachusetts was a large apple farm, and each weekend, the Paine family would come from their home in Boston to work the farm and relax.

There was a tennis court across the dirt road where Bill and Sada loved to play tennis on the weekends. They both took long horse rides since Sada was also a very skilled horsewoman, practiced in steeple chasing, as a "hunter jumper" and fox hunting. Sada also taught Bill how to dance playing phonograph records such "Buttons and Bows," by Dinah Shore; "Red Roses For A Blue Lady," by Tepper and Bennett; "Tennessee Waltz," by Stewart and King; among other classics. Bill, however, preferred to slow dance with Sada to cowboy songs such as like "Cool Water," by Monroe and The Sons of the Pioneers.

In their private time, after a hard day of work, Sada was very helpful in educating Bill on how to get along in with the Boston natives. He was, after all, Irish, a group of people who had come to Boston by the hundreds of thousands after the Great Famine in Ireland. Bostonians, many of whom could trace their ancestry to the early 1600s, considered the Irish to be ill-mannered, and uneducated. Consequently, if you were an Irish man in Boston at that time period, you had to fight for respect. Bill thought this kind of discrimination of the Irish in Boston was ironic.

"We are all immigrants in America," Bill thought to himself.

In the 1950s, some people in Boston still had a negative attitude toward the Irish, which was caused by a clash of cultures that occurred a century ago. "The Great Hunger," or "an Gorta Mór," in Irish, was a period of mass starvation, disease, and emigration out of the country. In 1845, a potato disease in Ireland wiped out the potato crop, a key food staple for the Irish. Two years later over thirteen thousand Irish had landed by boat in Boston, overwhelming the existing population. Boston at that time was predominantly White, Anglo-Saxon, Protestant. It was run by descendants of English Puritans many of whom could trace their lineage back to 1620 and the Mayflower ship. The majority of the incoming Irish refugees were Roman Catholic. Upon arrival in Boston and, desperate for food and shelter, the Irish refugees took any unskilled jobs they could find such as cleaning yards and stables, unloading ships, pushing carts, and cleaning sewers. They immediately grabbed onto the lowest rung of society and waged a daily battle for survival as they clawed and climbed their way up the ladder called the "American Dream."

In Ireland, throughout the Famine years, between 1845 and 1855, one million people died and over a million emigrated to the United States.

Cultural and religious differences between the Irish Catholic refugees and Boston natives took over one-hundred years to be resolved. Bill O'Brien understood why, but he was a well-traveled man of the world, he had a big heart and an open mind.

As Bill made his way through Boston high society and the business world, he frequently experienced the kind of demeaning behavior that earlier Irish immigrants had to deal with. But, instead of bemoaning this mistreatment, or feeling like he was a second-class citizen, Bill used his creativity, optimism, and authentic love of people to overcome prejudice, win friends, and gain respect.

On June 16, 1948, in Millis, Massachusetts, the elite society of Boston, Chicago, and Los Angeles joined in friendship with Bill's family and normal working class friends who knew Bill and Sada. Over one-hundred guests were gathered for the wedding of William Howard O'Brien and Sarah Sergeant Paine on the Paine's Apple Knoll Farm in Millis, Massachusetts. The elegant ceremony took place in the beautiful garden overlooking the small lake, blanketed by the hundreds of apple trees, and red maple, oak and walnut trees. Spirited stallions and mares galloped in the wide stables below. Bill and Sada were truly, madly in love. He needed and wanted her as much as she needed him. In later years, on hearing Bill describe his wedding to Sarah Paine in Millis, he said, "True love is the greatest cosmetic."

The beginning of one of the greatest love stories.

Just Married.

BILL O'BRIEN WOOL MERCHANT

After their wedding, Bill continued to pour himself into the business of becoming a Boston wool merchant for Draper and Company. He started first in the warehouse, loading, unloading, sorting, and passing wool up to the grader. It was dirty, backbreaking work to handle bales of wool every day.

The best way to learn about the international wool business was to first understand what wool felt like and smelled like. After work, Bill looked as if he has taken a bath in lanolin, a fatty substance found naturally on sheep's wool. The smell of lanolin was now permanently in Bill's nostrils, and he could never get used to the feeling of having it all over his body and face. Every evening, he was anxious to get home and take a hot-water bath.

Mike Bertolletti was an Italian wool grader who had worked for Draper for twenty-seven years, since the company opened its doors. He was Bill's supervisor and he taught Bill the secrets of the trade, such as where to look on the fleece to get the highest grade percentage, and how to distinguish grades of wool by their fineness. Fine Grade was used for worsted clothing mills, Medium Grade for blanket mills and Coarse Wool was for carpet mills. The length was also important, lengthy was staple for strength and sort was used for sweaters and felting quality. Bill was fascinated on how many variations in wool grading there were and how to understand what the mill buyers want.

Over the fall and winter the job in the warehouse was going well but Bill was anxious for a change to grow beyond a factory job. He knew he had to be patient and to prove himself.

As with many things in life, the opportunity came, but not the way Bill wanted. It was after the death of the company's wool buyer out in the Western United States. He passed away right in the beginning of the shearing season.

It was almost the end of his shift when Paul Draper walked up to Bill and said, "O'Brien, remember when I talked to you about opportunity?"

"Yes sir, I sure do," Bill responded. "I am willing to wait for as long as it takes."

"Well, you don't have to wait long. I want you to be our wool buyer for the Western United States, effective immediately."

The smell of lanolin in his nose and on his wool-dusted hands suddenly vanished, only to be replaced by that familiar racing heart and quickening of the pulse. The adrenalin was kicking in.

Bill only managed to say, "Thank you for the opportunity, Mr. Draper. I'll take it."

Bill and his bride Sada had only been married for eight months when Paul Draper promoted him to buyer. In driving to California to start his work, the newlywed couple had the opportunity to extend their honeymoon. They drove to Bill's parents home in Santa Monica where Sada was to stay with them. She got a job as an assistant Kindergarten teacher while Bill had to travel the Western United States.

For Bill, he was in the right business at the right time in the right place. In the years to come, as the United States military and civilian population grew more than anytime in history, the demand for wool sharply increased.

In the United States alone more babies were born in 1946 than ever before. This was the beginning of the so-called "baby boom." In the next twenty years the baby boom continued to increase by the millions, until the mid-sixties, when the boom finally tapered off.

Knowing that Sada was safe and happy with his parents, Bill headed for Bakersfield, a large wool growing area, where the first shearing was to start. It was late morning on a Sunday. Spring was in full bloom, hundreds of farms spread out across the open green fields a region that hosted abundant green and leafy vegetation. Central California truly was the most productive farmland in America. Bill had his hands full, and in California he had to look long and hard for good wool-buying deals.

As he entered the quiet streets of this inland city of northern California, he whispered, "What a beautiful country!"

He had never been in Bakersfield and had no idea where the sheep ranches were. One thing he knew was that he was hungry. The sign read "Los Rancheros Restaurant" and since he loved Mexican food he stopped for lunch. A large group of Mexican men were having a joyful time, drinking beer and singing Mexican songs. The pitchers of beer were leaving the table empty to be replaced with full ones, while the men were laughing and talking loud. The Mexican men all wore boots and cowboy hats. Bill was impressed with the energy and approached their table where he immediately was asked to sit down and join them by an older man who was a bit less intoxicated from joy than the rest. He offered Bill beer and food. It helped if you knew Spanish, and fortunately Bill did.

"This is a happy group," Bill commented in Spanish.

"*Sí. Es nuestro día libre. Estamos celebrando nuestro fortuna de alimentos para tener trabajo y familias saludables.*

Mi nombre es Jorge.

(Yes, it is our day off. We are celebrating for our good fortune to have work and healthy families. My name is Jorge.) he responded as he raised his glass.

"Qué tipo de trabajo hacen ustedes?"

(What kind of work do you do?") Bill asked his new-found friend.

Jorge, a middle aged, tall and thin dark haired man. "We are sheep shearers, you know, we shear sheep." He simply said, now in English with a Spanish heavy accent.

Bill could not believe it. He had just driven into Bakersfield alone, not knowing anybody or anywhere you could find people who work with sheep, and the first place he stopped, he ran into Mexican sheep shearers.

Trying not to be too over-eager, Bill said, "I'm a wool buyer, new in town, and I am looking for the sheep ranchers." Jorge, raised his glass again, "You are in luck amigo. Me and my friends here, we know all the sheep farmers in the Central Valley."

Bill asked if he could go with them to meet some of the farmers.

"Of course amigo, we are going to work early in the morning. For now drink, relax and enjoy."

The Mexican sheep shearers enjoyed each other's company at Los Rancheros Restaurant in Bakersfield until early afternoon. They laughed and talked and sang their favorite Mexican songs. They were impressed that Bill, a Gringo vaquero, knew so many Mexican songs. Finally, the Mexican sheep shearers asked Bill, in Spanish, who his favorite Mexican composer was. His answer instantly, "Agustín Lara. And my favorite song he wrote is *Solamente una vez.*"

The Mexican sheep shearers, were amazed that this

Gringo, knew who Agustín Lara was. They welcomed Bill into their world of sheep, friendship, and Mexican culture. Before leaving Jorge told Bill, "Meet us outside this restaurant tomorrow, Sunday, at four in the morning. You can travel with us and learn what we know."

Thanks to these Bakersfield Mexican sheep shearers Bill found, just because he loved Mexican food and culture, he got to meet all the top sheep farmers in California. He travelled with them for weeks, camping out under the stars by night, and meeting sheep ranchers and placing wool orders by day. Bill's incredible success in buying wool in Central California was because he was right there, in the arena, as he tells it, as the sheep shearing happened, traveling with the Mexican shearers and learning the ropes. After spending a few weeks in Bakersfield, he travel through Colorado, New Mexico, Utah and North and South Dakota, meeting ranchers and sheep shearers, attending wool auctions, placing orders and packing wool to send back to Boston. He had become a top-performing wool buyer in less than half a year. Finally, after six months he went back to Boston where he reunited with Sada who had finished her teaching job and was back from Los Angeles. All the time Bill was away on wool business, he and Sada called and wrote back and forth constantly during his travels on wool business. Neither time nor distance could diminish their feelings for each other since that first day they met. Sometimes they didn't see each other for more than six months. Still they wrote and called. Bill and Sada's letters are stored, to this day, in two big footlockers in their Paradise Valley home, silent testament to their enduring love for each other.

SOUTH AFRICA, ELEPHANTS AND SHARKS

Bill was making a fortune in the wool business for Draper and Company. His sales volume across the Western United States was almost double his predecessor's.

After the buying season ended in the United States, Paul Draper decided to send Bill to South Africa and South America. Bill quickly agreed, but only if his beloved bride, Sada went with him.

South Africa is a beautiful country of coastlines that stretches along the South Atlantic and Indian oceans. It is a multi-ethnic society with a wide variety of cultures, languages, and religions. A year before Bill arrived, in 1948, the South African National Party imposed *apartheid,* an Afrikaans word meaning "the state of being apart," literally *"apart-hood."* It was a system of racial segregation in South Africa enforced through legislation by the National Party. Under apartheid, the rights, associations, and movements of the majority of black African residents and other ethnic groups were curtailed, and the white Afrikaner minority rule was maintained. Racial segregation in South Africa began in colonial times under the Dutch Empire. Apartheid legislation classified inhabitants into four racial groups, black, white, coloured, and Indian.

This was the environment Bill and Sada were thrust into. Bill ever understood why people treated each other differently, just because they looked different.

"Back in Uni High we all got along pretty well," Bill tells me, "Any disagreements were quickly settled on the schoolyard and that was the end of it. It kind of reminded me of my growing up in an Irish family."

Bill and Sada quickly fell in love with the temperate climate, the crisp air and the beautiful coastline that extended hundreds of miles from Richard's Bay east of Johannesburg to Cape Town in the southwest of South Africa, where some of the farms were located. The coastline extended in to parallel ranges of fold mountains creating a breathtaking topographic image of endless beauty. Inland from that lengthy coastline and before the Kalahari Desert is the plateau of the Great Karoo, South Africa's vast farmland.

Because of Bill's cheerful personality and unrestrained confidence, together with Sada's polite composure and striking beauty they made friends easily.

While waiting for new wool to arrive from the sheep ranches for auction, they enjoyed the countryside together. They became great friends with Norm Patterson, a car dealer originally from Austin, Texas and his wife Barbara, a woman of captivating beauty. Norm was multi-talented; he was a gifted photographer and an aircraft pilot who flew planes for the National Guard and the Red Cross. Norm was also a serious dancer and loved to tell jokes. He had his own plane and the four friends took long flights across South Africa countryside. They flew over blue waters dotted with yachts and fishing boats, and they marveled at the verdant hills, green plateaus, and long dirt roads trailing off into the horizon.

The four friends would go to Cape Town and Walvis Bay to attend the wool auctions and to meet the sheep ranchers. Cape Town is the gateway to the South African wine lands and it was just starting to earn a reputation as one of the great wine capitals of the world. Here the cultures of Africa, Europe and the East have met and mingled for over three-hundred-fifty years. Consequently the city is both ancient and modern, rich in colorful history and culturally diverse. Many of these ranchers also produced a great white wine which the two couples were grateful volunteers for the taste. Being a former Navy man, Bill also befriended several people in the small United States Navy base on Cape Horn. On the Navy base, he was permitted to measure the cargo weight of all shipments he send back home, which greatly helped his wool buying operation.

On weekends, Bill and Norm would play polo in Port Elizabeth. They were extremely competitive on horseback, and sometimes they forgot that this was only a game. Bill loved to go hunting as well with his favorite polo pony, named "Corvette." He and his fellow hunters would ride out to the African plains with their hunting dogs leading the way. They hunted wild boar, an extremely aggressive and ill-tempered beast that can be really dangerous when wounded. Also called a bush pig, the animal is a significant nuisance in the agricultural regions of South Africa, so the local farmers welcomed the hunters anytime.

Out in the open plains, Bill was to have a defining moment, one that affected Bill and his relationship to nature and animals for years to come. He was on a safari with a doctor and another wool buyer. An African guide led the three man deep in to the forest and they eventually found themselves walking along a broad river and through a bamboo thicket, with riffle in hand they followed their experienced, quiet escort. Suddenly the African guide signaled to stop and pointed to a direction ahead. Bill walked quietly, towards their African guide. Just outside of a clearing of trees some thirty feet ahead, Bill could not believe his eyes. It was a fully grown African elephant.

It was looking directly at Bill, not moving a muscle and

not making a sound.

Bill's heart raised with excitement, looking at the majestic animal, his mind overflowing with conflicting emotions. He slowly raised his rifle, placed it over his heart, tilted his head behind the scope, squeezed his finger against the trigger and then, he suddenly pause and muttered "I can not kill that beautiful animal," he lowered his rifle and walked away.

The African elephant raised his trunk and turned, heading back toward the trees in the distance. When Bill got back to camp, he paid the African hunter guide and told him that he didn't feel like hunting any more.

Two days later, Bill had great success at the wool auctions with strong buying orders from Japan and light competition from England, Europe and Russia. After the auction, a felt slipper manufacturer named Herman Beir gave Bill, on pure trust, a consignment of two hundred bales of a short fiber lamb wool for the felting industry. Bill thought to himself that night that he was very glad he let that elephant live, and that the good Lord was watching over him.

Bill and Sada made many friends, went to dinner with several South Africans, and met people who were in the wool, shipping, and banking business. Being tennis players themselves, they were excited to meet tennis professionals from the United States Tennis Team who were touring South Africa. Bill was thrilled when the head coach of the team asked him to be the local American team representative.

Their favorite beach was KwaZulu Natal on the northeastern coast of South Africa, because the surfing was great and the sea breezes were mild. They loved to relax by playing Canasta on the beach. But one Sunday afternoon, Bill lost five humiliating matches to Sada. He jammed the cards in the sand muttering unintelligibly, and swam a burning crawl hundreds of yards straight out to the ocean. Having cooled off from his embarrassing loss, he started to swim back to shore. He spied three teenager surfers in great shape who were also already heading back to the shore. Bill waved at them and swam. Suddenly, swimming five feet away from Bill, one of the teenagers shouted "Shark!" and in a flash the kid disappeared under water without a sound. Being a Frogman, Bill had swam in shark water many times, but this was the first disaster he had witnessed. Bill yelled to the other kids who started screaming with fear. "Keep your hands under water and don't kick or splash." He thought there might be a school of sharks and he didn't want to attract attention. The event was news in the paper the next morning.

Bill hasn't played Canasta ever since.

Back in Port Elizabeth. Bill was getting ready for a major meeting of sheep ranchers south of the Great Karoo. The Karoo area was familiar to Bill since it was similar to Arizona with very marginal vegetation desert in the summer and incredibly green, yellow and red the rest of the seasons. On a ranch in the Great Karoo, Bill first saw a magnificent hound, the African Rhodesian Ridgeback, a large, muscular dog also called African lion hound. They are known for being great watchdogs, even-tempered, and wonderful with kids. Originally bred in South Africa to hunt lions, the cross-breeding began with the Hottentots, a native race of South Africa, and the early Dutch, German, Dutch and Huguenot emigrants. The peculiarity of the Ridgeback breed is the ridge of hair which grows facing forward on his back in an extended diamond down his spine.

In the sheep ranchers' wool buying meeting in the Great Karoo, there was lots of talking and drinking beer. When it was time for Bill to do business, it was a serious matter. When you put down hard currency to buy wool, it is important not to make mistakes. For example, they were trying to sell bales of wool that where sheared after a dry, dust-blowing season, which wears out the wool. Bill knew that the best kind of wool to buy is during a wet, cool season when the wool crop is the best. He wanted to get a feel for the wool clips, but the sheep ranchers were just laughing and chatting. He suspected the ranches were liberally pouring beer to the buyers to distract them from inspecting the dry wool. He became annoyed by the behavior and left. He thought that wool was too important a business to be handling over alcohol.

The same Friday during the night, the news came in that England had just devalued the pound sterling.

"Devalued in relation to what?" Bill asked his Barkley banker.

"To the dollar!" was his answer.

The devaluation from $4.05 down to $2.80 dollars for one English pound.

This was incredible news. He fully understood the implications of the devaluation of the English pound sterling. With his knowledge of the wool industry and of international finance, learned in college and in business, he knew exactly what to do. It was highly risky. It could be a career-ending move for Bill because he had to act without getting permission from his director at Draper in Boston. But it also had the potential to be incredibly lucrative. Bill's idea was to use wool as a vehicle to ride the currency devaluation before the American markets opened up, but he had to move fast. Essentially, the profits from the wool purchases were fine, but he real earnings would be the difference in value between the two currencies.

The devaluation of the pound sterling against the dollar gave Bill a once in a lifetime opportunity to make an overnight fortune. But he had no authorization from the home office. So he decided to buy all the wool he could across South Africa.

He took a plane to Cape Town, and headed straight to the wool market. In those days, all communication lines closed down from Friday to Monday. The telephone, the cable companies and much business in South Africa had no communication with the outside world. This devaluation gave Bill the opportunity to buy more wool for the dollar. He was on fire that day. He started placing huge orders at the Cape Town wool market. Other buyers from other countries were taken aback. But Bill still wanted to buy more. He took a taxi back to the airport and caught a flight to Port Elizabeth, and bought more wool. Then he flew to East London and then to Durban and bought more wool. He would just place the orders and then head to the next wool market.

Bill could not wait for confirming orders from Draper.

His office manager knocked on the door of the bungalow, armed with stacks of several phone messages, all from his director at Draper, back in Boston. The phone messages all said the same thing: "What are you doing, call me immediately!"

When Bill called his director in Boston, the director was outraged.

"O'Brien, who gave you the authority to make all these wool purchases! Have you any idea just how much trouble you've caused traveling up and down South Africa like a lunatic?" His voice was angry.

The line somehow went dead. Bill didn't bother to reconnect the call.

After a couple of hours, Bill received a telegram from Draper and Company.

He looked at Sada and said, "Darling, this is it. Make or break time. Whatever happens, I love you."

"I love you with all my heart, Bill," she said.

Bill went to the dining room table. Taking a deep breath, he opened the telegram.

"Maintain all purchases."

The home office had realized what Bill had done. His instincts were right. He had done it.

As Bill tells it, he placed one million dollars in wool purchases across South Africa and made about four-hundred-thousand dollars in profits from the currency devaluation plus the normal wool profits. Bill's courage, his ability to move fast and negotiate faster, had made Draper a fortune inside of three days. Plus Bill O'Brien secured a big fat commission for his efforts.

Bill's favorite motto was: "I love chaos. There's so much you can accomplish when chaos reigns supreme."

It was time to head back to Boston. Bill and Sada said goodbye to their friends and they headed to Durban, where he chartered a cargo ship, The African Rainbow. Although it was a cargo ship, it could accommodate twelve staterooms in luxurious quarters. The African Rainbow's Captain Peterson was a tough looking Dane with a great sense of humor. The ship's mates and engineer officers ate with the passengers and were encouraged to be sociable with the passengers.

From Durban, Bill had the ship stop at East London, Port Elizabeth, and Cape Town. The crew loaded the tons of wool Bill had bought on his cross-country buying spree. Before embarking on the ship, he sold his two polo ponies, loaded three champion Rhodesian Ridgebacks, a male and two females.

The ship was scheduled to go to New York but since all the ship's cargo was wool, Captain Peterson agreed to change course to Boston. That also helped Bill get those Ridgebacks into the United States because the veterinarian could meet the ship and handle all the paperwork.

The twenty-one day trip home was uneventful. Besides the

O'Briens, the twelve staterooms were occupied by Seventh-Day Adventist believers, one German banker, Baron Von Tucher who had several oil paintings hidden from the Nazi's survivors of World War II, and Barton Mumaw, a ballet dance that was in several successful Broadway shows.

At last Bill and Sada were home in Millis. They were very happy to get back to their farmhouse in Millis and see Sada's parents and friends. Rhodesian Ridgebacks created quite a sensation in the New England papers and later, the hounds were featured in Life magazine. They gave one Ridgeback to Sada's parents and one to Paul and Marjorie Draper.

Bill, hunting in style.

Bill and Sada with young Wendy and Justin.

PERU, ARGENTINA AND
RHODESIAN RIDGEBACKS

After handling the cargo ship full of wool, Bill was told by Paul Draper to go to Peru and buy Alpaca. The Korean War was on and the Navy was taking the great circle route along the Aleutians Islands in Alaska to deliver troops. They needed lightweight jackets for the troops. Reflecting on his success in South Africa, Bill's entrepreneurial skills were sharpened and he found himself in the unique position to negotiate new terms. Bill suggested that he would go to Peru but wanted to pay his own way. He would offer the company the right of first option to buy, with all firm offers subject to a prompt reply. If Draper refused the offer, Bill would be allow to sell to other buyers. It was his way to start his own business while keeping his loyalty to Mr. Draper. Paul Draper agreed and Bill took the Pan American overnight sleeper bunk to Lima, Peru.

He checked in with Ambassador Harold Tittmann which was required by Navy during war times.

He walked around Lima for a few days to get familiar with the city and check out the huge docks in the Port of Callao, Peru's main commercial seaport just outside Lima. Bill decided he would use Callao, one of South America's few good natural harbors on the Pacific Ocean, for his Alpaca purchases in Northern Peru. For the south, he would use Mollendo and Matarani ports. He learned all this quickly because he walked the docks of each port, always asking the dockworkers about the how, where, when and what of all cargo going out of the harbor.

After a nice lunch he went to a pub where people are easy to talk to and learned that Arequipa, a southern city in the Andes, was the heart of Alpaca country. The city is surrounded by the Andes mountains in the eastand a mountain range of minor mountains in the South and west, while the Chili River crosses the town from north to south. The valley of Arequipa played a key role in allowing Arequipa to be the second most industrialized city of Peru, since strategically links the coastal and highland regions of southern Peru to the outside world. Bill made Arequipa his base for the next few years and managed his business between Arequipa and Lima.

There were eight Alpaca dealers in Arequipa and they all traded with the Inca Indians who raised and sheared their Alpaca Llama and various crossbreeds. The Alpaca dealers had Inca women who sat in a circle sorting the colors, black, grey, dark coffee, coffee, light coffee, light brown, tan and white. These colors were spun by hand into yarn. The mills spun them tighter for jackets, sweaters, and carpets.

Bill along with a group of Peruvians started a personalized carpet business. It created jobs and economic activity and helped Bill politically with the Peruvian government. It was also a very profitable business for Bill O'Brien.

He continued the shipments of Alpaca wool bales on the Grace Line cargo ships from Mollendo, the main port in the Peruvian southern coast and closer to the Pacific ocean. Exports like wool, textiles, fish and other Peruvian products reached the world from the port of Mollendo. Mollendo, also being a popular beach resort, had however a disadvantage because the water by the docks was shallow. The ships anchored off shore and each bale was hoisted aboard from the barges by the ships boom one at a time. In one of those times a bale was dropped in the ocean accidentally and Bill was amazed that it floated. It was the time that he figured out why most wool and Alpaca weighed more when arrived in Boston. During the long sea voyage to Boston through the Panama Canal, the Caribbean sea and the Atlantic, the cargo gained about two percent moisture.

His first shipment to Mr. Draper was two-hundred bales of Alpaca bought from a local wool warehouse.

Bill airmailed samples and lot numbers to encourage sales and to satisfy his bank line of credit and also to be with family as much as possible. He usually flew home when the ship departed so he could get the lots sold to the mills through wool salesmen.

In the spring of 1951, baby blonde-haired, blue-eyed Wendy Paine O'Brien was born into the O'Brien's family home in Millis, Massachusetts. Bill stayed as long as he could with Sada and the beautiful baby girl.

The next territory to explore was Argentina. However, doing business in Argentina under President Juan Peron, was difficult. The Argentine president charged a higher rate of exchange to the United States than he did to the French which, Bill thought, was not fair. There was such a wide margin that the French were buying the wool, repackaging it in France and selling it to the United States as a French product. Bill set up a Peruvian Trading Company to buy Argentine wool for Peru. While en route he sold the wool through Boston wool brokers and trans-shipped the cargo to the United States. The extra freight through the Panama Canal was more than offset by the favorable rate of exchange. Selling to the United States mills was easy because he could offer wool cheaper than all competitors except the French.

On Bill's final wool transaction in Argentina sending

wool shipments to Peru, that was the day the Argentine Senate passed a law excluding Peru from the exchange rate. It was purely a business decision, since Peru was importing more wool and paying less than other buyers. Bill had already legally booked a shipment to Peru and was loading it on the ship in the Buenos Aires harbor. But President Peron found out when Bill's cargo ship full of wool was departing, and he sent a platoon of Argentine soldiers down to the dock to stop the ship from leaving. Bill saw the Army platoon leaving, so he sprinted to the bridge and ordered the Captain that he could not take any more cargo and to shove-off immediately. The ship hoisted anchor and left, and Bill abandoned the rest of his wool cargo. He slipped off the back of the cargo ship and flagged down a taxi.

He didn't want to spend the rest of his days in an Argentina prison. Looking warily over his shoulder for Peron's platoon, as he went to the ticket counter, Bill bought a ticket and took the first plane leaving the country to anywhere; he didn't care where it was going Eventually he landed back in Millis safe and sound. A few days later, Bill received a visit from two men in suits from the U.S. State Department. They told him the State Department had received an angry call from President Juan Person's office, demanding to know where Bill's cargo ship was. The two men quickly determined that Bill had just been bringing wool legally to the American people, so the matter was dropped. That was a relief to Bill, but he never went back to Argentina, because he knew President Peron was one tough hombre.

When Bill and Sada O'Brien had stepped off the African Rainbow in Boston Harbor with their first three Rhodesian Ridgebacks entering the United States were glad to be back home. The dogs Bill had hand-selected, Tchaika, Caesar and Zua, were to be the primary breed line in America for the Rhodesian Ridgebacks under their kennel name "Redhouse Kennel." A year later, Bill had founded "The Rhodesian Ridgeback Club of America" which adopted the standard of the breed from South Africa and started working closely with both the Africa and Canadian Kennel Clubs. Prior to that time, some of the first people who owned Rhodesian Ridgebacks in the United States were stars like Errol Flynn and Robert Mitchum. Bill started his own pedigree book and, after several litters, he imported a couple of new top-blood Ridgebacks registered with the South African Kennel Club. Bill's breeds and breeding professors at the University of Arizona College of Agriculture, helped guide his breeding programs so the dogs would not become inbred like the Irish setter and the Collie had been previously.

Bill's Studbook for the breed was accepted by American Kennel Club when they recognized the breed in 1955, starting with Bill and Sada's Tchaika of Redhouse. Since that time, thousands of families have enjoyed the Rhodesian Ridgeback breed, and the dogs are valued for their loyalty, companionship, and intelligence. Besides his love for dogs, Bill loved horses. He was a member of various clubs and entered many horse competitions, especially horse jumping and long cross-country races. His only experience before the horse jumping competitions was limited to the U. S. Horse Cavalry where to get the feel of the horse, you had to jump fourteen-inch logs in the corral bareback and blind folder. It wasn't dangerous because those army horses knew more about jumping than he did.

Sada and the Ridgebacks on the African Queen coming home.

Bill and Sada in Boston with the Ridgebacks.

POLIO AND THE PROMISE

In the year of 1916, several cities in the U.S. were struck with an unusual epidemic. At first with chills and headaches, then paralysis from a joint suddenly stiff, to the entire body immobilized. Some people were unable to breath or swallow, and death followed quickly. In the absence of clear information from health authorities, the public panicked. Autopsies of the dead showed inflammation of the anterior spinal cord, and the disease got its name: poliomyelitis. From that year on there was not a single year that passed without an epidemic of polio.

By 1952, when the first vaccine was introduced, there were hundreds of thousands paralyzed from polio in every state. However it would require years of testing.

That was the defining moment that brought Bill and Sada closer together than ever before.

"It was a Sunday in April, 1952." Bill said, "We were at our home in Millis, Massachusetts. The Salk Polio vaccine had not yet come out. I was sitting by Sada's bed. Her body was burning from fever and she was crying out in pain. This was not the Flu. I was holding her hand and patted a wet towel on her forehead to bring her body temperature down. It was the second day that she was running a high fever. I told her if she still had a fever tomorrow, I'd take her to the hospital." Bill expressed his concern about the symptoms. He remembered that Sada managed to say a faint, "okay," before falling asleep. For Bill, the night was a sleepless one, as he sat by his wife's bedside, watching her turning and sweating.

By the morning, Sada's fever had broken and, besides the usual weakness after the trial of illness, she seemed to be fine. But Bill was not convinced. He once saw a horse with a fever and, although he ate his oats and hey, the horse would cough and had mucus fluid out of his nose and mouth. Bill noticed at the time that the horse could not bend his head to his chest to reach for his food, he had to lower his body in order to eat. The problem was a spinal inflammation, and Bill never forgot that.

The next morning, Bill greeted Sada with breakfast in bed. He had an idea.

"How are you feeling?" Bill kept asking Sada. He sensed that she was in pain.

"Better, I just need some rest." Sada said, coughing and blowing her nose. She was not convincing. He knew there was something wrong. That cough and the stiffness on her neck reminded him of the symptom of his horse. After a constant coughing, nose blowing and obvious neck pain, she said, "I don't feel well, Bill."

Bill said, "Do me a favor. Please lower your chin to your chest."

Sada struggled for a minute but she could not lower her chin to her chest.

Bill turned to her and said, "Sada, I'm calling the doctor." Bill was firm on his decision.

"Dr. Martin," Bill said over the phone to his family doctor, "my wife has all the signs having polio. Please come over to our home as soon as possible."

When the doctor, a younger man, arrived, he examined Sada thoroughly. He removed his stethoscope and stood up and stared at Bill.

"I think you are right," Dr. Martin said gravely. "I'm calling an ambulance right away. I don't know how you knew, but I believe she has polio."

The Boston Memorial hospital was about forty minutes away. On the drive to the Emergency Room, Sada was confused and turned to Bill.

"What did I do wrong to get polio? What will I do? How can I live with this horrible disease?

Her crying voice penetrated to the very core of Bill's heart.

As they settled into the hospital, Bill sat with her on the hospital bed, held both her hands, looked her in the eyes and said, "I promise you this, Sada. I promise I will be by your side for the rest of my life.

Tears ran on Sada's cheeks, "It is not fair to you. It's just not fair."

"Nonsense darling. I will always stand by you. For the rest of my life. This is my promise to you."

It was a moment of tender powerfulness - the incredible component that only perpetual love stimulates. The doctors at Boston Memorial said it would take about six months for Sada to recover. They added that, if Sada had arrived into the Emergency Room a day later, she would have been paralyzed for life. Thanks to Bill's keen perception, quick thinking, and decisive action, Sada was able to fully recover. The doctors asked Bill how he knew she had polio even before the doctors did.

As Bill had been trained by his parents, he just smiled and said nothing.

Together . . .

For Ever.

MOVE TO ARIZONA

Sada learned how to walk with a cane and, after much therapy, she was able to regain full use of her body from this awful poliomyelitis.

After Sada recovered, the young couple carefully considered their options. Their children, Wendy, now age six, and her little brother, Justin, were doing well. Bill's international wool business had enjoyed tremendous post-war prosperity, but man-made fibers were starting to gain market share. Bill saw plenty of opportunity in the wide open spaces of Arizona, and Sada wanted better weather to raise their two children.

After eight years in the wool business, Bill decided to move to Arizona and start a new life. He sold his wool business, their Millis home and small farm, and his horses, and they said goodbye to the Paines and to their friends and drove to Arizona with their two small children and a kennel of Rhodesian Ridgebacks.

The drive from Boston to Phoenix was three days long, and the kids were good passengers. Bill had some old University of Arizona buddies who now lived in Phoenix, and they showed him around the growing city. They rented a three-bedroom house with a horse stable on at the foot on Camelback Mountain.

From Bill's field research in the Valley of the Sun, he sensed that real estate was the future business in Arizona, "Once people discover the great opportunities in Arizona, and the weather, clean air, and the beauty of this state, they will be moving here by the droves," he often said.

Through his college friends and new friends he made, Bill was introduced to many Phoenix area business people and government leaders who were championing their vision of the future of a prosperous Phoenix.

One of the key Phoenix influential leaders took Bill, who had just been in town a few weeks, out to lunch with some long-time Phoenix business people to Jack Durant's restaurant, a very popular hangout for businessman and politicians. After what seemed to be a lively conversation about local economy, politics and growth, apparently the men liked what they saw in Bill O'Brien. He was a fresh face, new in town and therefore had no enemies. He was smart, articulate, charming, and good-looking.

"Bill," the leader said, "We want you to run for State Senator for your district."

"Thank you," Bill said respectfully," But why? I just arrived in town and I don't know anybody. Why should I run?"

"Listen, Bill," one of the other men said, puffing a cigar, "You'll meet everybody in your district because you'll be knocking on everyone's door. You'll know in a hurry what the major issues are. You'll help our political party fill the ticket so we don't get clobbered or embarrassed. And, as for you, if you're lucky, you'll lose," the leader of the pack said with a broad smile. All the men at the table laughed heartily and slapped Bill on the back. While he didn't agree with their motives, Bill couldn't fault their logic. He agreed to run and they agreed to back him.

Back in The Shedd, Bill told me he was lucky because he didn't win, although he didn't know by how many votes, nor did he seem to care.

"The power brokers were right." Bill said, stroking his chin, "I did meet everyone and I did learn what were the important issues. And I learned that everybody is one-hundred percent right from their own perspective, no matter what political party you are. But that experience taught me that it's better not to be the guy holding the cigar."

That was Bill O'Brien's last foray into politics. From then on, for the rest of his career, he would help those who ran for office to make Arizona prosperous and secure. He was a front line District Committee leader, a national presidential primary delegate, and a behind-the-scenes supporter of what he thought were the brightest and the best in Arizona and national politics.

Bill graduated from Cecil Lawter School of Real Estate, received his real estate license

and joined O'Malley Real Estate company on Central Avenue in Phoenix. On the top floors of the O'Malley Building, the seventh floor, there were dozens of lawyers' offices. Bill saw an opportunity, so he went from floor to floor and struck up conversations in the break room and lobbies, talking to attorneys in a conversational manner about the incredible growth of Arizona real estate. He wasn't being pushy, he was just letting them see him every day. People trust you if they see you around all the time. Gradually, the lawyers realized Bill was sharp, he even looked like an attorney. They started asking him what he knew about real estate. Bill said casually that he knew a guy who had a huge plot of land in Carefree, north of Scottsdale. The Town of Carefree was just starting to get developed. He could find out more the next day and let the attorney know. He continued talking to other attorneys as he made his way down the floors of the O'Malley Building. The next day, Bill would give the prospective client a sheet with details about price, location, size of property, amenities, and growth prospects for Carefree. He was so friendly and non-assuming that they felt comfortable around Bill.

"I will talk to my wife and let you know," was the common answer from the potential buyers.

The next day he revisited everyone and asked, "Oh, hey, what do you think? What did the wife had to say?"

With his friendly sales style, Bill was extremely successful selling lots. The deal was ten percent down and low monthly payments. After his rounds, Bill would walk each morning in to the O'Malley's offices with a stack of hand-written checks sticking out from his shirt pocket. He just left the checks on his desk for his fellow agents to see. Bill wanted the other real estate sales people to know he was successful, that he could hustle. Bill's goal was not to brag, establish his his reputation in real estate. Always the entrepreneur, Bill couldn't see working for someone else his whole life. His plan was to start his own business and have his fellow real estate agents join him, and they could all make money. Bill thought that the commission given to the real estate agents was far too low, and he wanted to change that. He fully believed that if you work hard, you should be rewarded for all your hard work, because you had the incentive and motivation to be a success.

Bill eventually saved enough money to buy a 1920s cottage in Midtown neighborhood in uptown Phoenix, on Central and Osborn. The owner had lived in the home since the day it was built, but she was elderly and was going to nursing home. Bill gave her a good price, a fair price, because he knew he could fix it up and make a profit someday. He was excited when he brought Sada to see their new home. Sada walked all through the cottage, checking the fixtures. She then took one look at her husband and said, "Bill O'Brien, You bought this house to sell it. This is not our home. I do not want to live here."

Bill was shocked for that was his real plan.

"Sada, I thought we'll stay here for a while before we get a bigger home," he tried to convinced Sada.

"I know you well, Bill. You're not going to be happy here without room for our horses. Besides, knowing you, someone will make you an offer that's like this much," she said extending her hand above her head. "Then we'd have to move all over again."

She was not giving in. Bill realized that Sada was right. One of Bill's many strengths is that he listens to Sada's advice and cherishes her wisdom. To this day, Bill calls Sada, "My Snubbing Post," which is cowboy term for a solid heavy wooden post in a horse corral that is used to train horses.

That was his first home purchase in Arizona. Of course he sold it quickly at a very nice profit, and it whetted his appetite and fueled his desire to start his own firm. There were just a few minor problems. He did not have enough money to start such a firm, nor did he have the customer base to support the business.

From the Roaring Twenties to the Depressing Thirties to the Frightening Forties to the Friendly Fifties, and now to the Psychedelic Sixties, any normal American would think that they've had enough of this century. Any normal person, except Bill O'Brien who had been through so many extraordinary events. He wasn't greedy, he just wanted to experience everything. And as he would tell his ten-year-old son, Justin, who loved to listen to his father's many stories and adventures, "Justy, I'm just getting my boots on."

In the U.S. Presidential Election of 1960, John F. Kennedy, a dashing, athletic, wealthy, Irish-American Roman Catholic Navy war hero from Boston, defeated Richard M. Nixon, a secretive, awkward, yet strikingly reflective Quaker Irish-American, who grew up in California. It was the first-ever televised presidential debate, and the power of the new electronic medium became clear. Television viewers thought JFK, with his youth, energy, and Irish charm, won the debate and that Nixon appeared unshaven and shifty-eyed. In the 1,037 days that President Kennedy served, he established the Peace Corps, launched the spirits of Americans to launch a rocket to the moon, compelled Khrushchev to remove nuclear missiles from Cuba, signed major civil rights legislation and a Nuclear Test Ban Treaty, and was assassinated on November 22, 1963.

Riding with Justin.

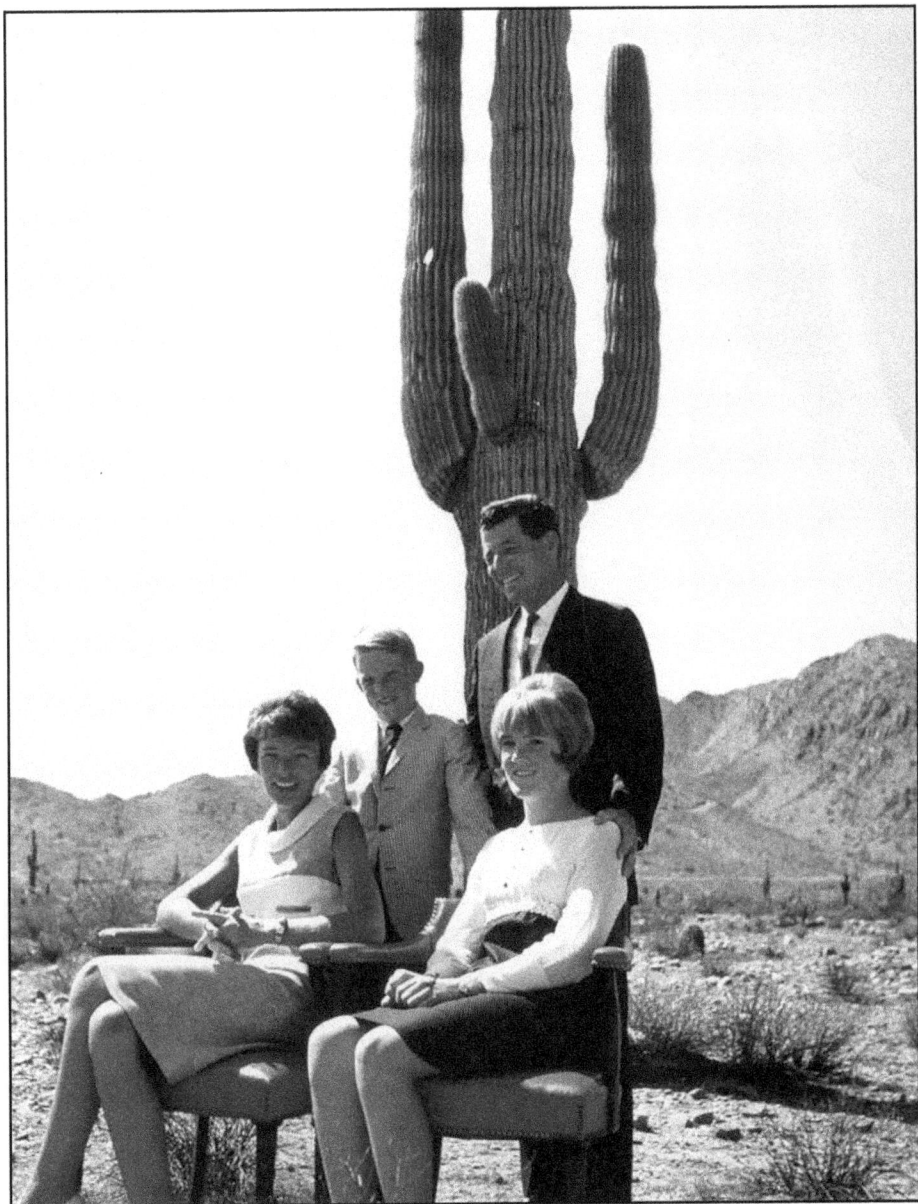

Making Arizona home.

PHOENIX IN THE SIXTIES

The Phoenix downtown area was the center of business and deal-making hub. During the sixties, Phoenix was a major agricultural center. The southern part of downtown, hosting warehouses and produce sheds, was a field overflowing with noisy energy even before the sunrise. Trucks jostled for space to load up fresh produce to be delivered to nearby towns, refrigerator cars and boxcars running down the streets on the railroad tracks loading the Valley's agricultural bounty to be headed both eastbound and westbound.

Phoenix was very much built around downtown and during the late sixties had begun to change dramatically, expending into its surroundings as the growth seemed to be unstoppable. The variety of the small shops in downtown were mostly locally owned and along with the family owned restaurants generated a vibrant business district . Entertainment was limited to the Fox Theater, the Orpheum and a few freestanding movie theaters. Both Greyhound and Continental Trail-ways operated busy depots in this area.

The Union Station was busy with sleeper cars carrying tourists and snowbirds from the Midwest, served by both the Southern Pacific and the Santa Fe Railways.

Eventually massive changes were undoing old agricultural arrangements as well as the transportation industry. Farmers expended their production to meet the demands of homegrown produce and the freeways arrived to ultimately replace the railroads.

Meantime, Bill O'Brien's real estate reputation increased greatly. He had a brilliant nose for finding undiscovered undervalued properties that were about to greatly increase in value. He believed that the number one law of real estate, Location, Location, Location, was too general. Bill had his own theories to identify great properties. First, for people to understand that there is growth of the urban areas and if any major economic project is coming, such as a big resort or new airport. Second, ready access to water and utilities. And third easy access to the property; are there paved roads, freeways, airports, property line disputes from neighbors?

Sometime around in the early sixties, Bill bought a beautiful home on two and a half acres in a rapidly growing area in an unincorporated part of Maricopa Country, Paradise Valley. Located on the north side of Camelback Mountain, and zoned for horses, the neighborhood still had dirt roads, septic only, county fire and police only, and private contractors for basic services. Local residents were afraid that, because McDonald Drive was on a section line, and the state liked to build major highways on section lines, this quiet rural area would soon become another Los Angeles-style suburb, complete with shopping malls and strip malls.

Bill joined the newly formed, Citizens Committee for the Incorporation of The Town of Paradise Valley, Arizona. The goals were to incorporate the area into a town, to keep zoning to a one house per acre minimum; to make it residential only, and to keep government regulation to a minimum. He worked to support the committee's efforts because he knew from his real estate sources just exactly what developers were planning in this precious valley. His one idea, however, to name the town, Camelback was voted down because there already was too much momentum toward the name Paradise Valley. Bill accepted the vote, but quietly thought to himself that the name, Camelback would have made a lot of sense, given that one of the most beautiful mountain in Arizona was right in their backyard. On May 24, 1961, the Town of Paradise Valley was granted, and the residents had done their job to protect this pristine area of Arizona.

While waiting for close of escrow, Bill and Sada would take their children, Wendy and Justin, now ages ten and eight, respectively, over to water the grounds and do cleanup.

"Justy, this is our new home," Bill said as he handed Justin a hose to water the fig tree. You'll grow up here with this magnificent view right in front of Camelback Mountain, which will become your personal playground. You can ride your bike everywhere and walk to elementary school. We'll take our horses out for early morning rides around Paradise Valley. And you kids will have all the benefits of country living, while being close to town."

It was around that time when Bill O'Brien, successful in real estate, but eager to build his own company, was searching for something new, something to grow with the times. He understood that there was no future working for O'Malley Real Estate. He started to dream big, envisioning a world beyond the O'Malley's Building. But Bill needed allies.

Bill O'Brien was restless, searching for opportunities, exploring possibilities. He visited countless Phoenix restaurants and bars, in search of business opportunity.

"I'd buy one drink, and nurse it for hours," Bill told me, "Money is too important to talk about if you've had too much to drink."

Soon he began making new contacts and friends. All his

life, Bill never had any difficulty making new friends. Perhaps it was because of his instantly likable personality, or his sense of humor or his desire to help others. Maybe it was his broad, heartfelt smile that, as I said before, seemed to extend beyond his bright Irish face. Always quick with a joke or a story, Bill was quicker to lend a hand, to learn something new, to share an idea that the other fellow would really enjoy.

From all the places he visited, it was one restaurant on Central and Camelback that he frequented the most.

He noticed, for the second day five man sitting on a table tucked in the far corner of the dining room, a room filled with the aroma of fresh baked cinnamon rolls and brewed coffee. They dedicated hours of talking, keeping notes and refilling their coffee cups.

"What are they talking about," Bill O'Brien wandered every time he saw the five, middle-aged gentlemen cornered in their private existence. The popular restaurant in uptown Phoenix was overflowing with business professionals. It was where Bill wanted to be, in this coffee-scented, bacon-smelling place which according to many people was their favorite eating establishment.

"Say, what do these five people do in that corner everyday?" Bill asked the middle-aged waitress.

"I don't know. All they do is talk about money and business," she answered as she was rushing to serve her customers.

The next morning Bill was waiting for the restaurant door to open. The sunlight timidly peeked from beyond the mountains, and the activity on on the streets was slowly turning the quietness of the night into the usual morning traffic commotion. The restaurant door opened allowing the breakfast-seeking customers to hurry in for a table. Bill O'Brien, first on line, knew exactly where he wanted to go, to the table usually occupied by the five.

"Sorry, this table is reserved," The waitress was quick to announce.

"Oh, yes, I am part of that group." Bill answered. He ordered his favorite breakfast, oatmeal with cinnamon, and waited. The five arrived, all together, and walked towards their table. Seeing Bill siting there they seemed perplexed. "Excuse me" one of them said, "this is our table."

Bill smiled, "You could join me," he offered pointing to the empty chairs.

The oldest guy, who seemed to be the leader of the group, was a thin, medium-height gentlemen. He looked at Bill and he burst into a smile. He was obviously amused about this guy sitting in his usual place.

"Why not? Let's let the schmuck sit with us," he said, as he and the other men sat around the table.

"Jewish!" Bill thought. He was happy about that, knowing that Jewish men are smart business people. The five of them, all dressed in white shirt and black slacks, sat around Bill, not certain if they were to talk business in his presence. "We are going to talk to this character for a few minutes and then he will go on his way." some of the five thought. "Kid, I like you." the man said looking Bill directly in the eyes. "What's your business? You look Irish. What's your name, Kennedy?"

Ever since John F. Kennedy was elected President, people saw a strong resemblance between Bill O'Brien and John Kennedy.

"Bill O'Brien," he said, "Call me Bill."

"Call me David," the man said, and he introduced Bill to the others.

They sat quietly for a few minutes, looking around Bill,

not certain if they were to talk business in his presence. Little did they know that Bill O'Brien was not likely to disappear. "Well, tell us about you. Why we should be so honored to have you," the youngest of the group, said sarcastically. Bill held the floor. He wanted them to know who he was and what he was capable of.

He had a direct eye contact with each one of the five, before looking right at David and said, "In answer to the gentleman's question, a wise man asked me once if I was looking for a job or an opportunity. I told him that I'm looking for an opportunity. That belief has served me right all my life. I'm sitting here, barging in on your group, because I want to run my own real estate company. I know Phoenix now like the back of my hand. I drive many miles a day in the Valley, looking for property, raw land, and homes. I know how to sell real estate, and I have the records to prove it."

The confidence and energy of Bill's voice held the gang of five fascinated.

"But I can't buy and sell it all, and I can't know it all."

Bill paused again.

"But what I can do is share with you, every Friday, absolutely current field reports of all the real estate action I see out there. I'll give you what I've got, and you can give me tips that I can run down for you."

"What do you want from us?" David asked, obviously impressed.

"Straight talk, right to the point. I like that," Bill responded. "You are investors, you have the money, and I have the knowledge on how to buy and sell. It is that simple." "But we do not even know you," one of them responded.

"Then what a great opportunity for all of us to get to know each other and make a lot of money," Bill responded quickly.

Bill made a good first impression with them and that was the beginning of a long and prosperous relationship.

He filed for the necessary business licenses and O'Brien Industries was formed.

As Bill tells me, "I still didn't have much money to spend, but I looked at it from an economist's point of view. I could see where Arizona was going, I decided I will buy and sell land like a commodity, like it was wool."

And he did, becoming Bill O'Brien, land mogul, leveraging land-holding after land-holding. Along the way, he ended up with a home in Paradise Valley With his wife, Sada, he bought the two and a half acres in a rapidly growing area called Paradise Valley that still had dirt roads and plenty of cows and hens in the yards.

Although his real estate business were flourishing, Bill O'Brien's business mind was restless .

Consequently, his son Justin tells me that Bill O'Brien seems to have hundreds of friends, associates, cowboy pals, and people who know him by name, all over Arizona. As a kid traveling with Bill, it always took an extra half hour to leave a restaurant, no matter where in Arizona they were.

As son Justin tells me, "Bill and I are both licensed single-engine pilots. We used to fly his Cessna 180 Taildragger plane all over Arizona, California and Mexico on cattle ranching or farming business, or for recreation. In fact, had logged hundreds of hours with him unofficially before I could drive a car. He still calls himself a Bush Pilot, which I take to mean, a pilot who can fly anywhere and land on anything if necessary. Bill has logged so many hours flying to and from Phoenix to his Eagletail Ranch in Harquahala Valley. The Cessna 180 Taildragger is like a pickup truck to him, and he's taken off and landed countless thousands of times. His landings are so smooth you could many times hardly know we had touched down."

Justin continued his story to tell me that they were flying the Cessna 180 up to the magnificent Navajo Nation to a small town called "Kayenta." The Navajo Nation is immense, extends into the states of Utah , Arizona and New Mexico – tens of thousands of acres of unparalleled beauty. Without really saying it out loud, they were kind of lost.

Bill looks down below and says, "Hey, let's land at that little place and ask them where Kayenta is."

They landed the plane and tied it down. A Navajo man sitting outside the café. Bill warned his son that Navajo was men are not very talkative in English. They walked over to the café and asked the Navajo man where Kayenta was.

"Here,"was all he said.

Bill and Justin walked into Kayenta Café to get some lunch.

All of a sudden there was a lady's booming voice in a Southern accent, "Well, Bill O'Brien, as I live and breathe. How are you, cowboy?"

It was Mary Alice Young, who worked for Senator Barry Goldwater, and she'd known Bill and Sada for years. It took an extra two hours to finish lunch.

THE PRACTICAL JOKER

Bill's invisible friend, Kartheen has been following Bill since he was four years old during the Roaring Twenties, during economic depression, the all-out world war and a booming economy. But mostly there were years of great adventures, particularly while buying wool in the southern states, in South Africa, and South America.

Bill and I were sitting in "The Shedd," in his Paradise Valley home.

"Kartheen is only four inches tall. He would stand on my right shoulder and sometimes whisper, sometime holler in my ear. He's kind of like what you Greeks call a Muse."

I smiled at Bill, admiring how deftly he compared his friend, what would you call Kartheen, more like a miniature Leprechaun to the Greek Muses, the nine Greek goddesses of inspiration in literature, science, song-lyrics and the arts. They gave artists, philosophers and individuals the necessary inspiration for creation and were usually invoked at the beginning of various lyrical poems, such as in the Homeric epics; this happened so that the Muses give inspiration or speak through the poet's words.

Bill continued, "I somehow knew that I was never supposed to look at him when talking. I knew that if I shot a glance at him, he would leave me forever. In fact, later on, I didn't even have to talk out loud. I only had to think, and he would get it. I haven't seen him in years, but I know he'll will show up when I need him."

"What about the Sunkist orange tree story. Does Kartheen know about it?" I asked.

"Oh, the Sunkist story," he laughed, "I can tell you for sure, Kartheen put that idea into my head."

As Bill tells it, his next door neighbor, John, loved his grove of Valencia Orange trees. He was so proud of them, and he was constantly pruning them and harvesting the oranges from February to late June. The weather in the Arizona desert produces some of the best tasting citrus in the world. The hot Arizona summers and cool winters in the desert produce a much fuller flavored product than consistently warm climates like Florida, or in consistently mild climates such as the California coast. You could always count on John to bring over to Bill and Sada a bushel of Valencia Oranges on every major holiday. John was right puffed-up proud of his prolific orange tree. Bill always appreciated the oranges from his neighbor, but every time he came over, with his fruity bounty, you'd have to listen to him talk about oranges for several minutes.

One evening Bill, Sada, and Justin were making plans for an Easter Sunday brunch, and they actually realized they wanted to serve sweet Arizona orange juice.

Easter Sunday arrived in all its revitalizing glory. In the early pre-dawn light, Bill and Justin, dressed in dark T-shirts, went over to, as their neighbor John always described it, "fabulous, grove of Valencia Orange trees." They carried two ladders, two stamp ink pads, and two custom-made rubber stamp Bill had made for him earlier in the week. They quietly crept over the neighbor's unfenced back yard and meticulously applied the Sunkist logo to each and every orange they could possible reach. The task took over two hours. Then, creeping back home,

Bill picked up the phone to call his neighbor John, and casually asked him for those wonderful home-grown oranges.

"Sure, Bill, John said, "I'd love to bring you a bushel of my oranges. I'll go pick them right now."

At that moment in the story in The Shedd, Bill bursts out laughing. He said that soon after the phone call, John showed up at Bill and Sada's doorstep with a big bushel of Valencia oranges. "John, These are Sunkist oranges, did you buy them from the grocery store?" Bill asked mockingly. The look of bewildered astonishment in John's face was the greatest reward Bill has ever earned as a gentle practical joker.

For Bill, practical jokes, just like his stories, yarns, tall tales, and one-man joke re-enactments, are a big part of Bill's life. He says that a really good practical jokes should be funny, original, and authentic, provide a pain-free ribbing, and nobody gets hurt or humiliated. Sounds just like Bill O'Brien's personality.

"What was your greatest practical joke?" I asked.

"Well, let's see," said Bill, tilting his cowboy hat up an inch or two, "I guess the one about the mountain lion."

He stopped for a moment and gave a boyish smile. He then crinkled his brow and titled his head to the right. Was Kartheen talking to him, I wondered, and then laughed myself. I was getting caught up in Bill O'Brien's mystical world.

"Well, I was supposed to be the fall guy, the butt of someone else's joke, but I wasn't about to take it laying down."

As Bill tells the story, he was a member of the Verde Vaqueros, a group of Arizona cowboys who go on a six-day ride across Arizona each year to raise money for charitable organizations. One time they rode into the Mazatzal Wilderness, a vast woodland of steep foothills covered with ponderosa pines, brush and juniper trees. The skillful riders had to endure the hills and the narrow, vertical-walled canyons before getting near the Verde River which flows through the Sonoran Dessert. The Verde Vaqueros, about a hundred horsemen, continued into the spectacular country of the Tonto National Forrest, which embraces almost three million acres of rugged country, ranging from Saguaro cactus-studded desert to pine-forested mountains beneath the Mogollon Rim.

The year was 1964. The horseman, after a long ride, settled down to camp life for the evening. The nights were full of fine food and drink, the soft, low conversations in the camp, punctuated by laughter and back slapping.

Everyone gathered around the campfire, and some Verde Vaquero members started shouting for Bill to tell a story. They knew Bill could tell a good story, and his over-acting on purpose made his stories even funnier. As he stood with his back to the blazing fire, he began to tell a story. Raising his hands and his voice, and making strong eye contact with his listeners. He told of an amazing Apache Indian who could tell intricate details of riders on horseback and pioneers on covered wagon trains traveling across Arizona toward California, just by putting his ear to the ground.

Right before he shouted out the punchline, a steaming hot, green, gooey pile of horse manure sailed out of the darkness and struck Bill's face, shirt, and worst of all, his white cowboy hat. It was just so spontaneous and literally came out of nowhere. The hills echoed from the laughter of the riders. Eagle-eye Bill caught a glance at the one who had thrown it, and still smiling, waved to his fellow cowboys, and vanished into the night.

The city of Payson was nearby. Bill got in his truck and drove to a ranch of one of his friends, the Pyle family. The Pyles were pioneers of mountain lion hunting. Bill greeted them and explained what happened and how he was humiliated in front of his Verde Vaquero pals. Bill had an idea on how to get back at that rude cowboy, that "Individual," as Bill called him. In truth, the worst name anyone ever heard Bill call someone was, that "Individual." As he explained his plan of semi-gentle revenge, they all burst out laughing. The Pyles enthusiastically whistled their pack of six husky bloodhounds into their truck. Then they supplied Bill with the pelt of a freshly killed, reeking, skinned mountain lion.

A little past midnight. Bill quietly walked into camp. It was a long day, and all was quiet except the thunderous snoring from the tents. He was silently dragging the pelt of the freshly killed mountain lion through each camp, outside the tents, inside the tents under the cots and on top of the bed rolls of guys who laughed the hardest at his embarrassing scene with the horse manure, around the campfires, up the horse trails, down to the makeshift mess hall. In the timeless justice of the practical joker, he left undisturbed the tents of the cowboys who were upset over Bill's horse manure plight. He fully rubbed and spread the scent of the mountain lion hide at the tent, cot, and bedroll of the cowboy who actually threw the steaming dung pile at Bill, and threw the hide under his bed.

The moment had arrived. Bill crept over to the truck and unleashed the hounds. Now you have to understand that bloodhounds were developed to hunt wild boar and deer. The bloodhound can pick up a scent that's up to twelve days old. Often called a "Nose with a Dog Attached," the bloodhound has a larger nasal chamber than most dogs, and they can detect invisible scent particles when on a trail. So anyway, those hounds picked up the scent immediately and, without even waiting for Bill to lower the truck tail gate, they vaulted over the back of the truck, bellowing as they ran after the scent of mountain lion.

It was complete chaos.

Men started shouting and hopping out of their tents barefooted and in their underwear. Cots and entire tents collapsed like there was a major earthquake.

Horses whinnied and soon every man was aware of the sound of those bloody bloodhounds from hell in the middle of the night. Following the scent, the dogs came close, then drifted away from camp, making turns only to come back and finally burst through the tents, some beds the hounds ran under and some ran over. The ensuing pandemonium of baying dogs and traumatized men was possibly one the funniest scenes in Verde Vaqueros history. It was even funnier because a lot of the men who were the most panicky were some of Arizona's richest sportsman and distinguished politicians, and successful business executives. These included an Arizona mayor, an Arizona Supreme Court Justice, doctors, lawyers, and a U.S senator.

As the members surveyed the catastrophic campground, they stood transfixed, watching the six-pack of hounds dash straight into the tent of "The Individual," the one who had thrown the manure. With their deafening bellowing, and barking, the bloodhounds swarmed around him and upended his cot. That pitched the tent completely sideways into a jumbled wreck of a camp site. It took a few minutes before he realized that the pelt was under his bed and a bit longer before he could do anything about it.

In the morning, "The Individual" came up and apologized to Bill about the night before. As has always been his nature, Bill easily accepted his apology and they both sat down and laughed and retold the story to each other again. He told Bill that this was the first time in his life that he was speechless, which was a rare thing to happen to a trial lawyer.

JACKRABBITS, SNAKES AND MUZZLE LOADER

"Well, this story would be a lot funnier if it wasn't my car," Bill said, with mock sadness, then a ironic smile. My son, Justy, was just a kid, about eleven years old, I think. I had just given him his own 22 caliber rifle, one I had bought for myself years ago. I had the stock and the barrel sawed off so it was a great kid's gun. We were itching to use it, so, anyway, we drove our tan, 1964 Chevy El Camino several miles down Greene Wash, south of Casa Grande, a place invaded by Tamarisk trees, also called Athel trees. That's a general term for several species of Old World shrubs and trees with scale-like leaves on very thin terminal twigs. They're invaders, really. These may have propagated by pieces of branches that wash downstream in floods and take root, or they may be seedling." Bill said, clearly very comfortable talking about Arizona vegetation.

"It is amazing how could he remember all this at his age?" I thought.

Natural washes in this region are hosted by desert ironwood trees. It was a hot summer day, on the bank of the dry wash, and silently, a large jackrabbit, just stood there sitting in that classic jackrabbit stand, body upright and ears flattened against his back, relaxing in the shade of a small bush. His buff-colored coat helped him blend into the arid environment, but it caught Bill's eye while he and Justin were parked.

"Justy, how'd you like to try your hunting skills?"

Justin said nothing. He was well aware that, while his target practice scores were high, his actual kills were low, and Bill suspected that his son was not really cut out for killing and hunting. Bill reached into the Chevy El Camino, took out Justin's modified, rifle, checked the ammo, and handed it to his son.

"Position yourself, put your elbows on the top of the hood of the Chevy, aim your rifle at the jackrabbit, breath and fire when ready."

The Jackrabbit seemed unhurried as if he knew who was about to aim at him. Justin was ready.

"Ready, Justy? Now take three deep breaths, aim and pull the trigger," Bill said.

Justin took three slow breaths and pull the trigger. They heard a soft metallic sound, Justin was watching, expecting the jackrabbit to drop on the ground. To his surprise, the jackrabbit simply blinked and hopped away.

Justin looked at his dad confused.

Bill just gave a sad smile and stared at his tan El Camino, then asked "Justy, do you have any gum?"

Justin thought to himself, "Again with the gum. What is with the gum?" but nodded his head "Yes."

He chewed it up quickly and gave the sticky wad to his father. Bill then reached over to the hood of the El Camino and plugged the small hole left from Justin's bullet with the sticky gum. Justin had shot his own family car.

"That's okay Justin, We'll get him next time."

Justin looked puzzled on how the bullet hit the car and not the jackrabbit and one thing was for certain that hunting was not his game. But this was not the worst feeling that haunted him for a few days--it was the image of the jackrabbit mocking him.

However, snakes were a different story. It was early spring on the Gila River. It had rained the night before in this land where seven inches of rainfall was considered a monsoon. A riot of colorful desert wildflowers and green shoots of grass vigorously poked their way through the rocky Arizona desert, searching for the gift of sunlight and air. Bill and Justin were horseback riding along the broad wash of the normally dry Gila River, north of Gila Bend, near their longtime friend Ralph Narramore's ranch. Known as one of the hottest places on earth, in Gila Bend this early morning there was a mild eighty-eight-degree breeze filling the damp air with the scent of wildflowers and creosote bushes. Justin was relaxed, enjoying the environment he loved and with the man he admired. Bill and Justin got off their horses and walked across the dry wash in the middle of the Gila River over to admire the view. Suddenly, Justin froze in his tracks. His heart was racing.

"Snake!" Justin shouted in a heavy whisper to his father.

"Ah, yes." Said Bill, with all the calm, dispassionate curiosity. "Looks like a Western Diamond-backed Rattlesnake. It's a big one, about six feet long. The Latin derivation is Crotalus atrox. Funny name, eh, Jus? It means Fierce clapper, you know, like the clapper of a bell. Now why do you think they compare a rattlesnake to a bell? It's the most venomous rattlesnake in the West, responsible for more bites and deaths to humans than any other rattlesnake species in United States"

"Are you kidding me with the snake lessons. I am about to be attacked by a venomous snake!" Justing thought. "Snake!" the twelve-year old Justin repeated, visibly shaken and not knowing where to run or fly.

"Okay, I got it. Don't move," Bill said.

Bill approached the rattlesnake very deliberately. He stuck out the heel of his boot and the snake struck out and tried to bite the tough leather heal. Then Bill just stepped on the rattlesnake's head, pinning him down.

"Just, use your knife and cut his head off.

"No way! That's a rattlesnake. I can't do this," Justin responded.

"Yes you can do this. Just cut it off." Bill said.

The six-foot-long snake was wrapping itself wildly around Bill's right leg. Things were getting serious. Justin's heart was pumping and he feared for both their lives.

"If you don't cut it off it will attack me, bit me, and poison me, and I'll die out here in the desert," Bill said, with amazing calmness. Justin definitely did not want to have his father die and he positioned the knife just behind the snake's head, where the venom ducts are, closed his eyes, and cut the rattlesnake's head off.

Bill buried the poisonous head and patted Justin on the back, "Good job. Oh, and for homework tonight, I want you to write me a two-page report on the Western Diamond-backed Rattlesnake. That way, we might learn how to stay out of the way of his bigger brother next time we ride out here."

Bill laid back on his chair, his eyes lighten up and after a pleasant laughter, he said, "Good times with my son."

Justin shook his head and said nothing.

The time had gone quickly, sitting in the Shedd, three hours gone already but I guess there was time for another story. Laughter really is the best medicine, and Bill O'Brien's stories are good for the soul.

"What about one more story, my friend," I asked Bill.

"Well," Bill started, acting as if he was being compelled to talk, "I was in a trap shooting contest at another riding club I belong to, Rancheros Visitadores, or maybe I was a guest of the Santa Barbara Trail Riders, in California. One of the highlight of the outdoor activities was the trapshooting contest. These are very competitive events, the participants are drop dead serious, and some of their shotguns cost thousands of dollars. Too serious, I thought. This sport should be fun. And I knew just how to open it up.

So, the first squad stepped up to the line. Two guys were shooting. Pow! Bam! Twelve shots and then the next team. Now these trap shooters are very serious. I learned from shooting trap that a shooter doesn't go, Aww, shucks, gosh darn it! when they miss. They just say to themselves, Next bird. When it was my turn to the line I stepped up with an antique, hundred-dollar, barely functioning muzzle-loader that not even the squirrels would take seriously, If you've ever shot a muzzle loader, it takes forever. You have to: Check for load and swab bore dry - Open breechblock to install cap/primer - Point in safe direction and close block - Clear channel by firing cap - Drop in powder or pellets - Place bullet in muzzle - Use starter to push bullet into muzzle - Use ramrod to seat bullet completely. - Install cap or primer. - Close block and put on safe or fire. - Fire! - Repeat the process to fire again."

"Oh, plus the paper wadding," Bill continued. "On some turns, I would forget that paper wadding and have to start over again, shouting, Now wait. Now watch. I also found that the front section of the Wall Street Journal works best. Something about the ink they use, or maybe the quality of the writing. As I loaded my rifle, I would theatrically start opening the middle of the Wall Street Journal, eyeing my competitors. I pretended to be drawn toward by an article. That drove them mad. The guys who know me understood exactly what I was doing and they started chuckling. The other competitors by now were crimson red and steaming and yelled, Come on O'Brien. We don't have all day.

Bill whent on with the story, "I raised my muzzle loader

and shouted, 'Pull," then it was "Pow! I blasted the bird to smithereens. Then everyone did another round. Then I went up again with my muzzle loader, and I started doing the same slow poke loading. At this point the trap shooters were screaming for my blood, ready to hang me by my thumbs, so I played my Ace card.

"I know the rules," said Bill, "I have my rights. I will voluntarily withdraw from the match, but only if you give me First Prize in the Muzzle Loader Trapshooting Championship, and declare me the winner in that category, and give me a trophy"

To a man, they all yelled their agreement and told Bill to go to the Trap Shoot judge, then, they went back to their real sport of trap shooting.

"By-the -way, you guys have fun. This is a social event and should be entertaining, loosen up." Bill said as he walked away.

Father and son.

The two amigos.

KARTHEEN, LAST HUNT AND
THE FIRST SOUTHWEST SBIC

"Bill, whatever happened to Kartheen?" I asked him. "Do you still talk to him?" My question caught him by surprise. He looked at me, through me and into the distant past of what must have been good memories of his childhood.

"Oh, yes, he's still here after all these years, but we don't talk as often now days," he said. "I haven't noticed him on my right shoulder anymore, though. I think we were so close that we just kind of merged into each other."

"He's been a big part of your life. He probably knows you better than anybody else."

There was an unusual vitality in his eyes and a wide smile "We met when I was almost four and have been pals ever since. He was a little guy full of adventurous things to do and was good at new ideas and at letters too. On our very first adventure I ran across the lawn naked and we were caught hiding in the bushes an hour and a half later. They were pretty perturbed because of kidnappers and asked who gave me such an idea. My newfound pal whispered Kartheen so I blurted out Kartheen did it! After that we talked a lot. Sometimes I mentioned his name around grownups just to perpetuate the notion with them that he really did exist. I could feel his presence off and on through grammar school especially when in trouble. This guy was as strong as the Boy Scout Oath. It sounds weird but Kartheen taught me how to get out of my body and have a good look at myself from a distance. It's easy after a little practice."

Justin politely reminded Bill that we already talked about the growing up years and that we wanted to move on to new stories. Bill looked at me and I simply said, "Enough for today. You need to get some rest." Knowing full well that if you ask a storyteller to tell stories you better be ready for a long meeting.

Justin went hunting frequently with his father, but always very reluctantly. It was a father and son bonding, and his dad was so much fun in the great outdoors that the young boy would go anywhere just to be with him.

One of Justin's last hunting trips with Bill, was on the opening day of dove season, near Buckeye.

In the early morning light, Bill and Justin were standing a few yards apart amidst a broad thicket of native willows, cottonwoods and mesquite trees. Bill was ready to bag his limit of birds. Justin just wanted to be with his Dad.

Suddenly, a plump, white wing dove landed on Justin's shotgun and just sat there. As the bird courageously sat on the barrel of the astonished Justin's shotgun, they stared at each other. Justin thought it was as if they made a secret pact: "I will pretend to shoot you and you just fly like the heck out of here."

That was the unspoken deal. The white wing dove seemed to nod acknowledge at Justin, and he flew away. Justin fired, missing by yards as agreed, at the dove as it flew into the morning sky south toward Mexico.

His father saw all of this and finally understood. He knew that his son had always had some kind of special relationship with animals, especially birds. When the O'Brien family's parakeet flew out into the desert and landed on the top of a tall Eucalyptus tree, Bill asked Justin to go get the little bird. Justin just held up his finger and cooed the blue parakeet until he landed on the boy's finger. Bill realized that Justin would really rather learn how to fish than to shoot, so that became their father-son sport.

Although his real estate business was flourishing, Bill O'Brien's business mind was restless. In 1965, he founded the First Southwest Small Business Investment Co. The business was federally licensed and regulated by the Small Business Administration. The idea was to participate in certain small businesses that needed money to grow by providing equity capital, long-term loans with low interest. The financial help for companies not strong enough to obtain credit through normal channels helped many businesses to grow and created many new jobs. The small business Bill's investment company helped included a boat marina, fly spray manufacturer, electronics plant, air conditioning contractor, real estate development, tennis resort, trucking company and many more. In the meantime, Bill and his sales team sold hundreds of one to five acre parcels to people who wanted to own Arizona land for investment, recreation, micro-farming, or retirement homes.

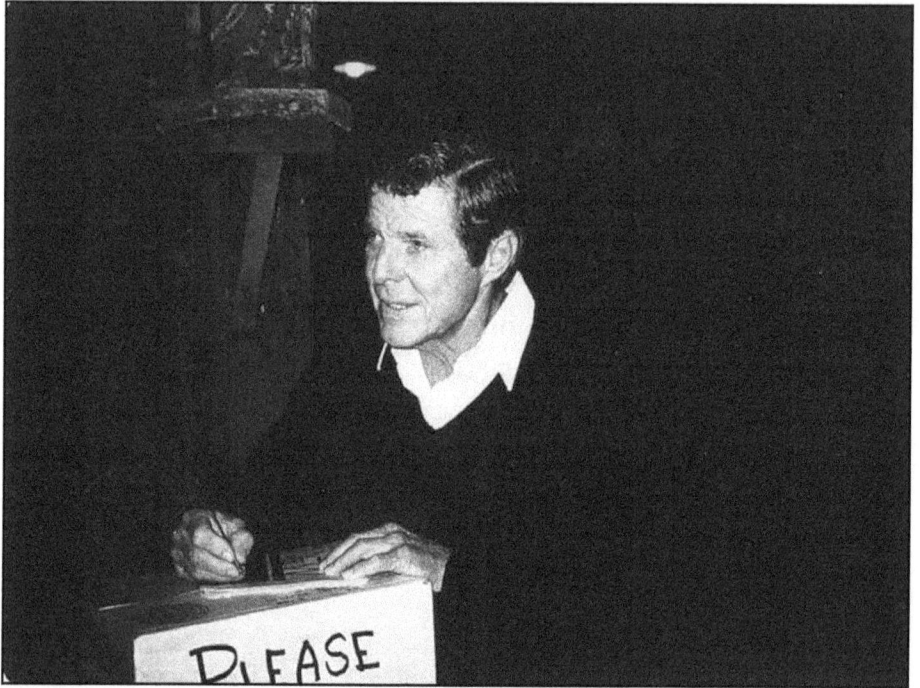

Planning the next venture.

ON THE TOP OF THE MOUNTAIN

It was after the spring of 1968. Sada walked by Bill's side as they climbed the narrow trail on the way up the mountainside. Her walk was strong and her ascent up the mountain effortless. She had made an amazing recovery from the life threatening diagnosis she had received a few years back. Naturally, Bill had chosen the most difficult path up the mountain.

The sun had began its descent into the western horizon and the earth was fragrant after the morning rain. They walked between giant saguaros, prickly pears, jumping cholla and wildflowers before reaching a steep, almost vertical slope. Sada went first and slowly found herself about ten feet up an extremely steep surface. She was a few feet from the top when Bill, climbing right behind her, noticed her legs trembling and knew that Sada was afraid of falling.

"I am right behind you, darling." Bill assured her, sensing her fear and terrified of the thought of his wife falling. He moved closer to her and pushed her up with his left arm while he carefully attempted to secure his own weight with his right hand, enabling him to find a sure footing on the soft surface.

Sada, a medium-height, thin-framed woman, made Bill's task to push her upwards easier. He was an experienced climber and he knew that, before making a move, he had to think about where his feet were going next. His right hand was used to support his weight, his left arm pushed Sada. Suddenly, one of his feet, unable to handle the weight, gave in and he slipped dropping rocky dirt downhill.

Sada heard the noise of falling debris. "What is happening?" her voice was frightened.

Bill quickly recovered his footing. "Nothing's wrong. Erase the fear from your mind." Bill tried to assure her that all was fine. "Just keep your body close to the rock face and do not look down."

He knew that keeping your body close to the climbing surface decreases the distance you have to move to get to the next hold and increases the effectiveness of your footholds. Dagga, their Rhodesian Ridgeback, had taken another trail and waited on top of the steep climb. The gleaming sun, touring the wide open sky, was near the end of its journey for the day.

"We are almost there, darling," Bill assured Sada.

After their steep climb, Dagga joined to walk along. Bill held Sada's hand to ease her walk on their way to reach their familiar spot on the top of Camelback Mountain. The gentle breeze was a welcome element as they stood on the peak of the mountain overlooking the entire Valley of the Sun.

They sat down to rest and once again, watched the Arizona sunset, and this was a particularly breathtaking one. The sun was now halfway behind the western mountains, its rays dispersed on the entire horizon, brushing the endless sky with a blaze of fiery orange and red colors.

"God, I love this place," Bill whispered.

Sada leaned her head onto his shoulder, "I am so happy here. I want to stay here for the rest of my life," she said without taking her eyes from the sky.

The sun was about to set as Bill and Sada stood up, rested and ready to go back before darkness fell.

"Come on, Dagga! Let's go down," Bill yelled.

The big, brown dog looked skeptical as if trying to say, "You're crazy, I'm not going that way!" He wiggled his tail and ran the other way to take the easier path down.

"Maybe we should go that way as well," Sada suggested.

"It is much longer and it is getting dark soon. The trails are dangerous after dark." Bill advised that they go back the same way they came.

On the way down and after passing the steepest parts, Dagga was there, waiting for them. Only a bit further to go.

There was one more steep part. Dagga hesitated and stayed behind.

"Come on, boy, let's go," Bill pleaded. "Here, Dagga. Come on, boy."

Bill stood below. Dagga seemed perplexed as he looked down at Bill.

"Come on, jump. I will catch you." The dog looked at him as if to say, "Are you kidding me now? I am eighty pounds and you are a little guy.

"Come on, boy," Bill insisted.

In a leap of faith, Dagga barked once and then hurtled himself off the cliff down to his rescuer. Bill caught him by the chest and legs, and both man and dog tumbled down the dusty trail, boots and paws splaying wildly. Bill's white cowboy hat flew off and landed cockeyed onto a barrel cactus. Bill stood up trying to dust off his clothes and his injured pride.

Seeing nobody was really hurt, Sada was amused at the site of her cowboy husband and her huge Rhodesian Ridgeback hound recover from their dance in the dirt.

"Sometimes you think you are superman, William O'Brien," She said laughing.

Bill smiled as Dagga ran away, barking in protest and probably thinking, "That man is crazy."

They arrived back at their home at the foot of Camelback Mountain. From their back yard, they looked up to the top of the mountain where they had just climbed. Bill and Sada O'Brien loved the peaceful environment in their home and neighborhood. They were happy and content that they had bought this home five years earlier. It was a great place to raise their children, Wendy and Justin, who were then eight and seven years old.

Bill and Sada. On the top of the world.

WENDY THE ARTIST, HER STORY

It was after Easter Sunrise service, in 1967, the family came back to their family home. It was good for everyone to be together. Thirteen-year old Justin was home from his second semester as an eighth grader at Robert Louis Stevenson College Preparatory School for Boys, in Pebble Beach, California. Although he missed his parents and his sister, Justin was so glad that he could go to one of the finest college preparatory schools in the country. The education was fantastic and Justin loved it. The sixties were difficult years, with the Vietnam War, the drugs, the racial tensions. It was really hard for Sada to lose her son for five years, from Eighth Grade to Senior Year, but she understood that education was the key to success.

That morning was one of those glorious spring mornings in Paradise Valley. The stunning colors of ultraviolet-blue jacaranda tree tops surfaced against the vibrant blue sky and blended with the golden-yellow overflowing leaves of the paloverde trees creating a resemblance of a Matisse painting. The fragrance of blooming flowers seemed to be extraordinarily pungent, as if they knew how precious little time they had to share their gift to the world.

Bill was sitting on the back patio of his home reading his newspaper, next to him Wendy kept doing her favorite pastime activity, she was capturing the colors of the nature on her drawing paper. Wendy was fifteen-years old. Bill took a break reading his paper to marvel at his daughter's painting. He looked at the trees, the mountain and the sky, then he checked Wendy's drawing and confirmed what he always knew - Wendy was a great artist.

"Wendy, what do you want to be when you grow up?" he asked.

"Oh, Dad, I am just trying to find myself," Wendy replied. Bill smiled thinking that every person at that age will probably have the same answer.

"What did you want to be when you were my age, Dad?" Wendy asked.

Without any hesitation Bill responded, "I wanted to be a cowboy back then, and I still want to be one! So, Wendy, I see that you are getting really good at painting. You are an artist. All through life, other opportunities will come your way and you should take advantage of some of them even thought they are not related to art, and they may even change your lifestyle. It won't make any difference because you will still be an artist."

Wendy looked at he Dad and smiled, "Then I want to be an artist for the rest of my life!"

He then realized just how much his fifteen-year old daughter, Wendy, had taught him about art and artists, ever since she started finger painting at six months old! And now his own daughter was blooming as a teenage artist as she and her generation hurled through this changeable, turbulent world of the sixties. Life was a lot harder for his children than it was for Bill, even though he grew up during the Great Depression.

Bill O'Brien never forgot his conversation with Wendy. Years later when he was putting on an exhibition with dozens of Wendy's painting in the great hall of the Irish Cultural Center in downtown Phoenix, it was the first time he had seen her art all together in one room. He noticed they were all different styles - what incredible range she had. Bill finally realized what Wendy had meant years earlier when she said, "Oh, Dad, I am just trying to find myself."

Bill now knew she didn't mean she didn't know what her career was going to be. She knew she was an artist and always would be. The artist in Wendy had been searching for the medium, and the style, and the subject matter most suited for her artistic abilities, sensibilities and interests. Each of her pieces of artwork was a distinct experiment: oil paintings, pastels the difficult water color paintings, charcoal, pencil, fine-line etching. The subject matter was across the spectrum: from still life, animals, portraits, abstracts, nature, scenery, humor, to reproductions of masters works to experimental post modern art. All subject matter, media, and styles combined to illustrate the amazing range of Wendy Paine O'Brien, the artist.

While looking at Wendy's collection, Bill's eyes stopped on a multicolored flower painting, yellow, blue, red, violet, trying to force a smile, it took a herculean effort to hold back the tears. He reminisced about that glorious morning in the back patio and he tried hard to keep the brightness of the face of young Wendy intact, when she was announcing the urge to be an artist forever, but his mind was overwhelmed with the memory of the darkest day of the O'Brien family.

Wendy suffered from manic depression, or what they now call bipolar disorder. The illness is a brain disorder that causes unusual shifts in mood, energy, activity levels, and the ability to carry out day-to-day tasks. Symptoms of bipolar disorder are severe, and the malady has affected people all over the world since the age of the Egyptians and the Greeks. The problems with the illness are different from the normal ups and downs that everyone goes through from time to time. Bipolar disorder symptoms can result in damaged relationships, poor job or school performance, and even suicide. Today, thanks to more therapeutic counseling and medicine, bipolar disorder can be treated, and people with this illness can lead full and productive lives.

The treatment methodologies used to help Wendy had limited effectiveness because the diagnostic analysis was evolving. Some days she would be doing better, her prolific art projects stimulated her soul and she felt alive. But other days, in a deeply dark and disturbed mood, she would shut her blackout curtains on all the windows of her house in the Encanto district, lock herself in her studio, turn a spot light on a canvas, the only light in the house, and sit down to paint. Working with brush, palette, pen, ink and watercolor brushes, she would paint happy daisies and cheery scenes of nature, flowers, trees, landscapes, and animals. Ultimately, in addition to this debilitating bipolar disorder, she suffered from paranoid schizophrenia and anxiety attacks, a perfect storm of mental stress. Toward the end of her life, she called Justin and asked that he take her to the hospital. Even after weeks of counseling and treatment, she eventually slipped into a place where neither hope nor help could reach her.

Heartbreakingly, on Mother's Day, May 11, 1980, Wendy, who loved to paint art and nature, the talented artist who signed each work with a daisy, surely the simplest and sunniest of flowers, ended her life. Two months after joining a Baptist church, one month after marrying the long-time love of her life, and twenty-five days after her 30th birthday, Wendy fought her last battle with depression. Before she took her life, she left a note to her parents and her husband, "I love you dearly but I want to be with God." Throughout her struggles, Wendy Paine O'Brien was still the very definition of an artist, a free spirit, one who sought solace in beauty, form, and color.

One year after Wendy's death Bill, Sada, and Justin O'Brien founded the Wendy Paine O'Brien Foundation. The purpose was to raise millions of dollars to create the Wendy Center, a behavioral treatment facility to help emotionally disturbed young people overcome their bouts with despair and anxiety. At the time, adolescents with drug or behavioral troubles were just sent to psychiatric hospitals, half-way drug rehabilitation treatment centers, jails or home, where they would just fall back to their old ways. The Wendy Center's goal was to provide counseling and appropriate medicine, but also to teach the emotionally troubled young people how to study, balance their checkbook, drive a car, make their bed, and behave properly in public.

Bill O'Brien uncharacteristically, does not talk about that often, but when asked he would say, "We wanted to catch these youngsters before they slide down into the depths of despair." When Arizonans were presented with this idea and the story behind it, their hearts opened up and the money poured in, Bill organized dozens of fund-raising events for the center. They raised millions of dollars. Good Samaritan Hospital System agreed to manage the center. Along with Sada and Justin he got the center started and since Bill is a smart man and knows his limitations, "I don't know anything on how to treat those kids, I let the experts handle that, but I am always looking for ways to get them money," he would say.

The building started out small, with a few rooms inside an existing hospital. The knowledge, care and treatment of these youngsters has grown exponentially since the center was built with private funds. The Wendy Center eventually had its own campus, team of doctors, counselors, and medical staff, and a regionally accredited Grade 5 to12 school whose students have gone on to Harvard and other top colleges. Since the Wendy Center opened in 1984, according to the executive staff at Banner Behavioral, tens of thousands of young people have come to the Wendy Center, received life-changing therapy and treatment, and have gone on to live happy productive lives. When Wendy took her life, Bill, Sada, and Justin could have just tried to move on with their lives. Instead, they turned grief into action, and the world is a bit better for it.

Wendy, So young, So beautiful.

Breaking ground for the Wendy Center.

CAMELBACK MOUNTAIN:
THE HUB OF THE VALLEY AT RISK

In the late Sixties, people from around the country began to discover the beauty of Arizona. Visitors noticed that Arizona was more than hot summers, red rocks, cactus, and Mexican food.

Anyone living in the Valley of the Sun knew that Camelback Mountain, besides having a landscape of natural beauty, knew that it was a popular outdoor activity spot for both area residents and visitors. As the Valley of the Sun continued to grow, Camelback Mountain served as a distinguishing symbol for the city that has grown up around it.

The first time Bill O'Brien saw Camelback Mountain, he immediately understood that it was the region's most prominent landmark.

"It's like the hub of a wheel," he would tell out-of-town guests "You'll never lose direction, and you'll know just where you are, if you always keep track of the Camel's back."

Camelback Mountain has always been a visual reminder of the dynamic tension and delicate balance between the man-made landscapes and the remaining wilderness of the Old West. What attracted visitors here, and to live here, was the wide open spaces. But that space was being increasingly threatened by new urban growth and expansion.

In the decades-long quest to maintain the natural beauty

of Camelback Mountain, many people, organizations, schools, and agencies became involved. The community rallied around Camelback, and their efforts serve as a role model for other groups trying to preserve open spaces and natural landscapes. Little did Bill O'Brien know that one day, with the help of his business partners, community leaders, and the tireless efforts of the local residents, he would play an important role in ensuring that the top of Camelback Mountain would remain forever undeveloped.

However, despite various efforts to preserve its natural beauty by limited development, Camelback Mountain was in trouble.

There was a grass roots effort called Save Camelback Mountain Committee, that had been lobbying government and business leaders to stop development of any kind higher than 1,800 feet elevation.

One of Bill's friends Don Dedera, the popular columnist for the Arizona Republic newspaper, had told Bill how Camelback was in danger of becoming overdeveloped.

"From what Don told me," Bill said, "I imagined tough looking guys in dark suits flying into Phoenix in the heat of the summer, hell bent on buying the top of Camelback Mountain." The rumors placed restaurants, fashionable hotels, and flashy nightclubs right at the top of Camelback. And, worst of all, a huge aerial tram, like the one in Palm Springs with its hideous wires scarring the side of Camelback, carrying tourists from the foot of the mountain all the way to the top. "What a disaster! I had to do something, but what?" Bill told Sada. She became angry.

"Can that really happen? Who would do such a thing?" Sada demanded to know.

"Just the aerial tram alone would be an unbearable

catastrophe for everyone in Paradise Valley," Bill said. "You know how loud the tramway's cable house is in Palm Springs. Here, it would echo throughout the valley."

Sada responded firmly, "All of this could turn this beautiful place into a circus. Bill you have to do something."

Bill thought about what life would be like for the residents of Paradise Valley if the new investors had their way. But what could he do? He was just one guy.

That evening, John Hughes, Bill's attorney, boxing partner, and college roommate of Bill's, arrived before dinner. Sada cooked a delicious cowboy dinner of Ribeye steak, salad with ranch dressing, baked potato, and strawberry shortcake, and the two old friends had a chance to reminisce about the good old days at University of Arizona. The talk shifted to Camelback Mountain. An idea started to form in Bill's effervescent mind but he said nothing.

He rose at four-thirty the next morning. He was anxious to ride Sunup, his three-year-old trusty Quarter Horse up to the top of Camelback Mountain. He led Sunup southeast across the north base of Camelback, heading for the east tip, the tail of Camelback. Horse and rider were absorbed in the cool and calm of the early morning mist and the chance to warm up before the ambitious climb ahead. The ride from the east side of the mountain was both challenging and spectacular. The steep climb and rocky, unstable ground made it a bit difficult for Sunup to find sure footing. Sunup was an extraordinary rock horse. At the steepest part of the mountain, near the top, Bill jumped off and walked Sunup who was good and lathered up by then, up the slope.

As a quiet picture of stamina, determination, and an appreciation for natural beauty, horse and rider stood proudly on the top of Camelback Mountain. The rising sun slowly illuminated the red boulders of the mountain, as the increasing daylight revealed the unfolding majestic views of the entire Valley of the Sun. Sunup snorted proudly, apparently aware of his athletic ability. Bill softly patted his horse on the neck, cooing at Sunup in that low, murmuring voice of his.

"Man, what a sight!" Bill said as he looked across the Valley and his house below.

The early-morning hikers stood silently, frozen in their tracks a few feet away. They were dumbfounded to see this cowboy on a horse on top of Camelback Mountain. Some hikers looked up to the sky, as if they imagined horse and rider flew down like the mythical Greek hero, Bellerophon, riding the winged horse, Pegasus.

Years later, Bill would say, "That was the most beautiful view I've ever seen. I could see as far as Apache Junction, Buckeye, and the McDowell Mountains."

Bill took off his white cowboy hat, swept the moisture off his brow with his red cowboy bandana, and stood next to Sunup to enjoy the view. He said a small prayer to God to give him strength for what he was planning to do to help save Camelback Mountain. He glanced once again down at his Paradise Valley home. He got back up on Sunup and they started back down. As Bill and Sunup treaded carefully down the eastern trail of the mountain, he recalled Sada's voice whispering in his ears, "They cannot turn this beautiful place into a circus."

Going downhill was dangerous, even for a seasoned cowboy and rider like Bill. At any time the horse could slip and fall. Because of the steepness of the trail, Sunup wasn't able to bend his head down far enough to see the ground, he had to secure his steps by instinct. Theirs was a partnership of mutual trust and respect.

When Bill returned, the children were already at Kiva

Elementary School and Sada was in her crafts room making Christmas wreaths for a local charity auction.

"Did you enjoy your ride?" Sada asked, "How was the view?"

Bill sensed that her tone of voice was incredibly deliberate and firm. Her voice reminded Bill of his mother voice whenever she said, "And I mean it."

Bill knew right there in Sada's crafts room that he had to make a decision. He was reminded again of his hero, President Teddy Roosevelt, who once said, "Do what you can, with what you have, where you are."

"Sada," he said with great deliberation, "I'm developing an idea that will stop anyone from building anything on top of Camelback Mountain."

Any other person would think Bill was crazy, but not Sada. After more than twenty years of marriage she knew just how extraordinary he was.

"That's my Bill O'Brien, the man I love."

Bill jumped full-speed into his mission. An early riser all his life, Bill says that his best ideas always come to him at four in the morning. He knew that he couldn't bear the thought of a nightclub and gondola on the top of Camelback Mountain, one of God's most beautiful creations. He knew that there had been grass roots movements among politicians, residents, business leaders, school kids, and others to stop development in the higher elevations of the mountain. Senator Barry Goldwater, Congressmen John Rhodes and Moe Udall lobbied hard in Congress but met with resistance. Fund raisers were held, but they couldn't raise enough in time, and the campaign was stalled. There were too many land owners, both public and private, on the mountain. It was an ecological, legal, social, political, and economic mess.

It was the summer of 1966. As the early morning sunrise gently dispersed its light over the mountain slopes, Bill glanced across the street from their home, at the foot of Camelback Mountain and there was the old Paradise Valley Racquet Club that had gone bankrupt a couple of years previously.

Just then, he thought, "I'll find some partners, buy the old Racquet Club and turn it into a world-class tennis resort. My only condition would be that we'd all have to agree to donate the twenty-six acres to the Save the Camelback Mountain Committee so nobody can every build on top of the mountain. That'll work! Thank you, God, and, by the way, good morning to You."

His plan was taking wings.

Bill formed a company called Camelback North to raise money and buy the bankrupt Racquet Club and its land that extended over the top of Camelback Mountain. He found a great team with real estate professionals Russell Jackson and Vic Jackson and Heitel . They met frequently to devise the master plan. Conveniently, the old Racquet Club property was finally coming up on the auction block at Phoenix City Hall the next summer. Bill declared that, since he had the most experience at auctions, he would handle the auction and win the bid.

After closing the deal, they would then turn the the property into a world-class tennis resort, complete with a list of movie stars and celebrities, tennis superstars, and nationally known politicians. For the remaining other twenty-six acres of the property that went nearly vertically up Camelback Mountain, they would donate to it to the City of Phoenix and the "Save the Camelback Mountain Committee," or whatever they were calling it then. Bill's private mission would be to keep all construction off of that precious mountain top. That way, all who visited Camelback Mountain could enjoy the splendor of that magnificent view.

After weeks of meetings with the Camelback North team, Bill was finally ready for the auction. The night before the auction, Bill O'Brien invited his attorney and old friend, John Hughes for another of Sada's fabulous dinners. The two men talked final strategy and what to do if Bill actually won the bid for the old Racquet Club property. There would be a lot of contracts to sign putting the new tennis resort together.

On Tuesday, July 5, 1966, before sunrise, Bill laid on his usual couch for his regular half-away creativity session. In Bill's ever-active Irish mind's eye, he imagined those tough guys from back east already in the auction hall lurking in the corner with their briefcase full of cold cash. They were wearing their dark glasses, black wool Fedora hats, and double-breasted black suits. They were scowling and snarling like lions at the "local yokels," hungry to devour the top of Camelback Mountain so they could build their nightclubs. That did it. Bill had seen enough. He opened his eyes and vaulted off the couch.

Sada was in the kitchen and had Bill's favorite Mexican breakfast was ready, "Huevos Rancheros."

"Good morning, darling." Bill said.

They hugged and kissed, and Sada said smiling, "How's my favorite cowboy?"

"Sada, we're all set for the auction," he declared. "I'm going to get that fifty-six acres and Russell and I will build that fabulous tennis resort. Plus, I'll forever put a stop to any ideas about building a nightclub and aerial tram on top of Camelback Mountain. If anyone tries to get in my way, why, I'll knock them on their..."

Bill paused, remembering his father's insistence on a strong vocabulary and to avoid course language. He looked lovingly at Sada, and continued "...err, place where the hip meets the saddle!"

The Family, in their home by the Camelback Mountain.

"VIEJO AMANCEER"
("Ol' Sunup)
By *Bill O'Brien*

He was only a Spanish pony,
That roams the rocky peaks,
He grazed upon the meadows
Drank water from the creeks.

He was known among the cowboys
As one you'd like to ride
For he could catch the fastest steer
On any mountainside

He was Sunup to all who knew him
And when given his fill of mas
He'd run with his soul like the wind
In the race called the 100-yard dash.

Not many could fine a first place
On the dusty road called a track
"Cause Sunup had the running grace
That put him in front of the pack.

He could walk a very narrow trail
From sunup to sundown
And never miss a step or fail
To return you safe and sound.

Life was but a game to him
For which he had a knack
He liked to have his belly scratched
And sometimes farther back.

How does one say goodbye
To a friend of so many years?
To think that this friend could die
Would cost too many tears.

So out to the range for the last time,
Where we had those very good rides,
To look at our sunset together
"While we stand side by side"

"Viejo" I thought as I loosened his cinch
And pulled off the old brown saddle,
He is just as tall by every inch
"My God what a hell of a battle"

I looked at him and he looked at me
With his blaze face to the sun,
And I thought of all the good times…
"Damn we had lots of fun."

I pulled the bridle from his ears
And said my last good-by,
Like thanks again for all those years,
Better go before I cry.

Sometimes I think I see him
Out on the range alone,
And in my dreams I hear him
Trotting his way back home.

Years have passed, my bones are tired
And my hair has turned to gray,
But just as a priest remembers his prayers'
I'll remember Sunup today.

Best Friends.

"Attitudes," was Bill's favorite expression.

"Attitudes"

The longer I live, the more I realize the importance of
choosing the right attitude in life.
Attitude is more important than facts.
It is more important than your past;
more important than your education or your financial situation;
more important than your circumstances, your successes, or
your failures;
more important than what other people think or say or do.
It is more important than your appearance, your giftedness,
or your skills.
It will make or break a company. It will cause a church to
soar or sink.
It will make the difference between a happy home or a
miserable home.
You have a choice each day regarding the attitude you
will embrace.
Life is like a violin.
You can focus on the broken strings that dangle,
or you can play your life's melody on the one that remains.
You cannot change the years that have passed,
nor can you change the daily tick of the clock.
You cannot change the pace of your march toward your death.
You cannot change the decisions or reactions of other people.
And you certainly cannot change the inevitable.
Those are strings that dangle!
What you can do is play on the one string that
remains – your attitude.
I am convinced that life is 10 percent what happens to me
and 90 percent how I react to it.
The same is true for you.

226

CITY HALL AUCTION

It was scorching hot even early in the morning that July 5, 1966. Bill arrived at what is now called "Old City Hall" in downtown Phoenix on Washington Street. As he climbed the steps into the five story building, he suddenly stopped at the top of the steps. Bill gazed in admiration at the two beautifully sculpted sand-colored "Birds of Phoenix" on both sides of the entrance. They were half-embedded into the sandstone entryway. Bill thought they looked like they were struggling to fly, rising from the ashes.

Inside, the big brass doors to the auction hall opened, allowing the crowd of eager buyers in, looking for deals.

The big hall filled up fast. The place was packed, standing room only. Bill spied his buddy, John Hughes walking in, and gestured imperceptibly for the attorney to have a seat in the third row. Pretending not to know him, Bill sat in the fourth row, just behind and to the left of John.

Under Bill's guidance, the plan was that John Hughes was going to be doing the actual bidding for the property. Over the last decade since Bill arrived to Phoenix, he had earned quite a reputation in the Phoenix real estate market. He was a master at spotting overlooked, undervalued commercial property. Those in the know understood that, if Bill O'Brien was interested in a property, then that property must be worth another look. Consequently, at the auction that morning, Bill didn't want to be seen as an interested buyer in the old Paradise Valley Racquet Club, because the bidding would go sky high. So his plan was to have his attorney pal, John Hughes, a widely respected attorney in town, do the bidding, as if it was on his own.

Everyone took their seats. The room was noisy but the atmosphere was cordial. Bill studied the list of commercial, residential, and government properties, It was going to be a long day. He was at the City Hall auction for only one reason, to buy at auction that old tennis club, with its thousand-foot-wide belt of land that stretched east to west behind the property up over the top of Camelback Mountain to the southern side of the mountain.

"The strategy in any auction, Bill said, "was to study your main opponents. You have to see how high they're able to go, and act as if you willing to go higher. Also, never let them know what you really, really want."

Before the auction, Bill had done his homework. He knew at least three investors in the Valley were interested in the property, but he had a general idea about their upper bidding limit. But Bill also knew they would probably just subdivide the property into residential homes, and that meant their total revenue of the deal would be fixed. The real threat would be if there were any out-of-towners rolling in to the auction, armed with briefcases full of cash.

Dozens of properties were auctioned off. It was getting really hot outside. People in the crowd fanned themselves with the auction catalog. The air conditioning in the big hall was on maximum and strained to keep the room cool. At last, the Paradise Valley property came up on the docket. Bill pretended to be bored. He lowered his cowboy hat and studied his boots. Quietly, he lifted his head and peered around the room looking for possible competition.

Bill spotted the three possible competitors around the room. But wait. Who were those guys off to the side? They were obviously from out of town. Who on earth wears black wool three-piece suits in Phoenix in July? Was it possible that Bill's nightmare vision of tough guys from back East were here to grab the mountain top so they could build their atrocious nightclubs? The sight of those guys really got Bill's "Irish up," as they say. He was boiling mad inside, but he kept his cool on the outside, just like a good poker player. Bill quietly raised his right cowboy boot and tapped John's chair in front. It was Go Time.

The auctioneer, a real pro who knew his business, swiftly described the details of the fifty-six-acre property and then began his tongue-twisting, blizzard of words banter. Auctioneers talk fast in that, rhythmic monotone because the idea is to hypnotize the bidders, to lull them into a frenzy through a conditioned pattern of call and response. Their speed also makes the buyers believe there is a sense of urgency. Auctioneers typically earn a percentage of what they sell. So, by talking fast, they sell more in less time and they make more money.

As Bill tells me the story, the auctioneer opened the bid at $200,000 to keep the numbers easier to follow.

The auctioneer announced the opening bid starts at two-hundred-thousand dollars.

"What am I bid? Do I hear two-hundred-twenty-five thousand?" the auctioneer tongue was flying.

"Two-hundred-twenty-five thousand" a man cried out and raised his red bidder number sign from back of the hall.

"Two-hundred-fifty-thousand!" someone off to the side shouted, raising their sign.

"Three-hundred-thousand!" yelled a businessman up front.

"Three-hundred-twenty-thousand!," a well-dressed woman

in a middle row said.

The tongue-twisting, storm of words blasted out from the auctioneer's larynx and frantic bidding went back and forth. About four bidders were barking out numbers, raising the bid ten-thousand-dollars at a time. It seemed that was going to take some time, and suddenly the pace of the bidding started to slow down.

"Three-hundred-sixty-thousand," the man off to the side boldly said.

All of a sudden, one of the dark-suited men on the side stood up and stiffly raised his red numbered bidder. He stared menacingly at the other bidders and bellowed, "Three hundred-eighty-thousand-dollars!"

It was as if he believed a husky-throated voice alone could thwart all who dared challenge him.

Silence filled the room.

"Three hundred-eighty-five-thousand-dollars," the man off to the side finally said, but not as boldly as before.

"Three-hundred-ninety-thousand-dollars" the Easterner in the black wool suit said with a smirk. He must have thought that these local yokels were trying to nickel and dime him with chump change, five-thousand bucks at a time.

More silence in the hall. Then nothing.

Bill subtly scanned the room, studying the other bidders for the property. It looked like all the other four contenders had dropped out. The crowd sat straight in their seats, straining to watch the action of the two remaining bidders. Bill tilted his hat down and scrutinized the face of the Easterner. He watched as the man turned to consult with his cronies.

Bill sensed that the man in the three-piece wood suit was near his limit.

Then, Bill quietly wrote something on a piece of paper and

taped it to his right cowboy boot. He then tapped his boot on John Hughes' chair in front. Feigning a stretch, John secretively looked back and saw a handwritten note taped to the bottom of Bill's boot

"Stand up and shout out to the world, four-hundred-and-fifty-thousand-dollars! Do it now!"

Bill lowered his boot. John got the message.

Just then, the broad-shouldered John Hughes sprang to his feet, triumphantly raised up his red sign, glared at the man in black suit, and thundered out, "Four-hundred-and-fifty-thou-sand-dollars."

The man from back East rocked back on his heels. He feverishly consulted with his, cronies as Bill imagined them, and they started shaking their heads. The auctioneer made a deep sigh of relief. He was grateful to hurry it to a conclusion. There were still twenty more lots he needed to move today.

"Four-hundred-and-fifty-thousand-dollars." the auctioneer shouted sharply, accelerating his voice to a faster speed. "Going once, going twice, going three times—Sold. Next item…"

They won! Bill O'Brien and John Hughes had done it! There would not be any nightmarish idea of a noisy nightclub and a garish gondola clawing its way to the top. Bill and Russell Jackson now could begin to build their world-class tennis ranch at the foot of Camelback Mountain. The top of Camelback Mountain, this wondrous natural gift of granite and sandstone, would be saved forever. And best of all, Sada would be thrilled with her Arizona Irish cowboy.

"Happiness is riding my Mesquite." Sada Payne O'Brien.

Mothers Love. The most precious love of all.

232

THE MAN AND THE MOUNTAIN

Bill and his partners' plan to donate the twenty-six acres up to the top of Camelback Mountain to the City of Phoenix was soul fulfilling. But he now had to come back down to earth to solve big challenges to build the tennis resort. He needed an architect to design and develop the lower slopes in a way that would be compatible with its natural beauty. He also needed to find a tennis powerhouse personality who could attract top tennis pros, movie stars, celebrities, and world leaders.

He decided to visit his big sister, the actress Jane Bryan, now Jane Dart, who lived with her husband Justin Dart in Pebble Beach, California.

"When I was at my sister's place," Bill said to me during one of our numerous interviews in The Shedd, "I told her how we bought that old Paradise Valley Racquet Club and about my plan to save Camelback Mountain. I shared with her my vision of a tennis resort nestled right in the side of one of the world's most dramatic red rock settings. I told her that we would provide celebrities and leaders tennis lessons, clinics, and seasonal tournaments. I then asked if Jane knew John Gardiner."

John Gardiner was the tennis resort owner of John Gardiner's Tennis Ranch in Carmel Valley. The resort was a haven for tennis enthusiasts, and a popular destination for Hollywood movie stars, celebrities, tennis superstars and top business and government leaders.

Jane was actually a good friend of John Gardiner and told her brother that people would go there for a week or two to learn how to play from top tennis pros. So Bill asked his sister to drive him over to see Mr. Gardiner. Bill insisted to just drop him off that morning at the front gate and not to introduce him or use any of her considerable influence. Bill had to make the deal with Mr. Gardiner on the strength of its merits.

"As Jane waved me goodbye," Bill said, "I walked the long, winding driveway. I remember it was lined with those horizontal-shaped Monterey Cypress Trees. Then I saw Mr. Gardiner talking to one of his guests. I came over, introduced myself and we walked over to his office.

"Mr. Gardiner, you don't know me from Adam. But we just bought the old Paradise Valley Racquet Club in Arizona. I know you've played there in the past. It is thirty acres of land in Arizona in Paradise Valley on the slopes of beautiful Camelback Mountain, right in the middle of the Valley of the Sun. My partners and I want to build a world-class tennis resort with lots of courts, casitas people can buy, a great restaurant, pool, health club, top tennis pros, the works. We're looking for someone who knows all there is to know about running a top-tier tennis resort and making money with it. Everyone we talk to tells us that person is you."

Bill tilted his white cowboy hat upwards, which cowboys always did when they wanted to appear open, friendly, and trustworthy.

"Mr. Gardiner," Bill continued softly, slipping a bit deeper into his Arizona cowboy accent. "Here in Carmel Valley, you close your John Gardiner's Tennis Ranch in the fall and you open it in the spring, on account of the weather. The tennis resort we're gonna build on Camelback Mountain is a place that would open in fall and close after the spring. That means you could keep your tennis pros and top staff on payroll twice as long. Plus you'd make money almost all year round."

There was a long silence. John looked wistfully eastwards across the tennis courts to the Carmel Valley hills.

"Well, Mr. O'Brien," John Gardiner began to say.

"Call me Bill," he interjected.

"Well, Bill, what you have to say sounds interesting. I'll have to think about it and talk to my wife. I'll call you when you get back to Phoenix."

"I have a better idea," Bill said, ready to make his bold move. "Of course, please talk to your wife. This is a big decision that will change your life for the better. By the way, I have in my pocket two plane tickets, one for me and one for you, for a flight leaving this afternoon from Monterey Airport. You'll be my guest tonight at our home at the foot of Camelback Mountain, right across from the new tennis resort we want to build. We'll have a great dinner, and you can see for yourself firsthand just how incredible this place and this idea is. What do you say?"

How could John Gardiner argue with such a man as Bill O'Brien, a man with such vision, courage, and overwhelming Irish charm? This complete stranger, had walked into John Gardiner's Tennis Ranch, laid out a brilliant idea to build a first-class tennis resort in Paradise Valley, and persuaded John to come with him that afternoon on an airplane with plane tickets he brought with him.

John Gardiner said yes. They flew back to Phoenix that afternoon. Over a steak dinner Sada cooked, the final deal was sealed. In February, 1970, the Tennis Ranch opened its doors as both a resort and membership health club. It had 41 casitas, and larger casas, 21 tennis courts, including one on the roof of one of the buildings, an Olympic-sized swimming pool and beautifully landscaped grounds at the base of Camelback

Mountain. For years, the resort attracted Hollywood celebrities, international tennis stars, business leaders, and top politicians to the north side of Camelback Mountain to play tennis and have fun in the Valley of the Sun. World-class tennis pros would play there as well.

True to his word, in 1970, Bill and the partnership donated the twenty-six acres above the Tennis Ranch up over to the other side of Camelback Mountain to the newly established Preservation of Camelback Mountain Foundation. Thanks to the dedication of Arizonans like Barry Goldwater, Moe Udall, John Rhodes, Arizona leaders, countless residents, and, above all, the Valley high school students who held endless fund-raisers to save the natural beauty of the jewel of the Valley, the top of Camelback Mountain would be protected for ever.

When Bill O'Brien made the decision to be actively involved with preserving Camelback Mountain, he set up a meeting with the editor of the local newspaper. Now that Bill and his partners owned a thousand-foot wide band of Camelback Mountain land extending up, behind the old Racquet Club, to the top of Camelback Mountain, and down a bit on the other side, he told the newspapers that his partnership was going to donate the twenty-six acres to a committee that would never develop the land. This was quite literally the capstone gift that would hand the Save Camelback Mountain Committee the key to success.

Although the preceding efforts to save Camelback Mountain were essential prior to the involvement by Bill O'Brien and his partners, it can be said that it took the determination of a small group of people to actually secure the preservation of the Camelback Mountain.

It was a beautiful spring morning walking to the Shedd, as I looked in admiration at this agile, profound, complex ninety-two year old man. Bill O'Brien tilted back his cowboy hat, noded his head, and pointed to the top of Camelback Mountain and said, "There could have been a huge tram going up all night long to some bar and nightclub on top of the peak!"

Throughout his long life, the key to Bill's accomplishing his many goals, is the unbeatable combination of salesmanship, determination, definiteness of purpose and the assurance that he was doing the right thing for the benefit of many.

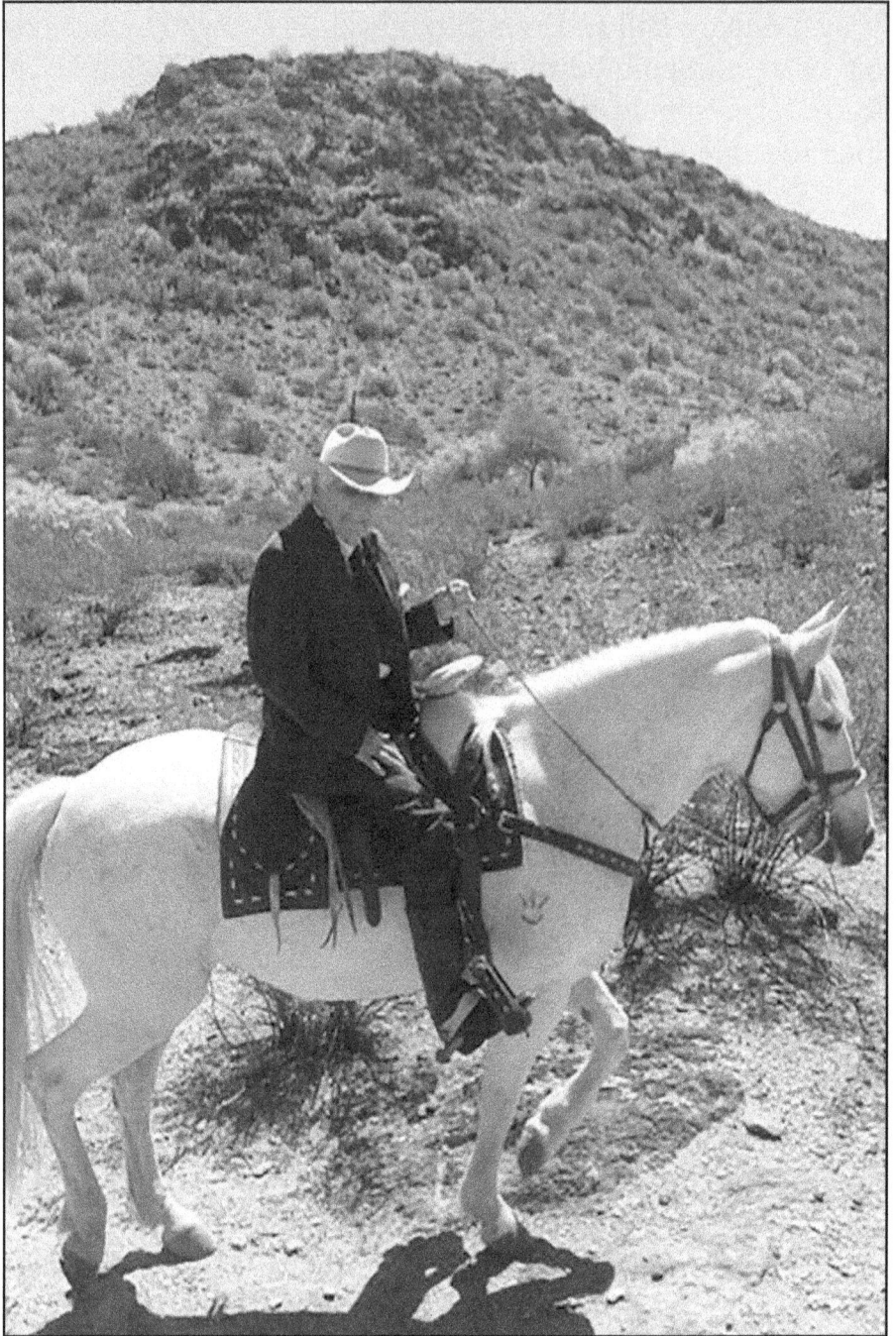

The Extraordinary Arizona Irish Cowboy.

EAGLETAIL RANCH

Bill O'Brien's Eagletail Ranch occupies thirteen percent percent of the land in Yuma County, seven-hundred square miles of cattle grazing rights you either own, lease, or have unfettered access to. The land is arid, low desert, an emblematic Arizona property where most people think that vegetation and wildlife is not possible to exist in land such as this. But Bill O'Brien is not like most people. He made this wide empty spaces west of Phoenix a great destination for people to live, work, cultivate and a shelter for desert animal and birds. The Eagletail Ranch is as remote as you could get in Arizona. Away from the city lights where the stars at night sparkle like jewels on a dark indigo blanket. The stars here are like you have never seen them before, Mars is vivid red, Jupiter stellar silver, The Big Dipper is an array of orange, blue and white and the moon bright yellow surrounded by the blue of the sky.

When the sun rises, it illuminates the great purple and brown wall of the Eagletail Mountains. The sun reveals Clanton's Well, named after Thomas Newton Clanton, a descendant of Ike Clanton who was part of the famous Clanton Gang in the shootout in the OK Corral with Wyatt Earp. Alongside it is Sada's Valley, named after Sada Paine O'Brien, for her endless contribution to this land. There's Sada's Wash and Red Tail Road, named because of the predominance of the Red Tail Hawks in the area. At the head of Sada's Valley there is La Tortuga Mountain, where

Sada had released several tortoises. In the lower range of the hill there is Cemetery Ridge, a sixteen-mile-long land where several prospectors worked the mines. On the west side of the Eagletail Mountain there is a magnificent volcanic cone that resembles a blacksmith's anvil. Its shear, straight cliffs on all four sides rise three-thousand-feet high and it is named O'Brien's Anvil, in honor of Bill's father James M. O'Brien, an earlier traveler to Arizona. The O'Brien Anvil is useful to the cowboys at roundup who use it as a guide to drive the cattle from all directions to the waterhole at the base of this massive rock formation.

There are many names on the Eagletail Mountain Range based on historical events and figures, like Spanish Fume, Courthouse Rock, Cortez Peak, Brownell Peak, and there is the Lost Frenchman Gold Mines, the legendary lost gold mines of Arizona discovered by Bill O'Brien when he was looking for cattle up a canyon. After further exploration there was discovered a forty-foot cistern through solid rock, a sixty-foot horizontal mine shaft and two graves.

If you happen to walk through those grounds with Bill O'Brien he will point out everything from the running waters, the mountain ranges, the holes dug by ground squirrels, the history of the trees, and every particular detail about this massive place.

Bill is a storyteller and he tells each story with a passionate voice, except when it comes to the story of his daughter Wendy. He loves this land of Harquahala and evidents of his love is that he scattered Wendy's ashes here along with many others who loved this amazing piece of land. It is where Bill comes to remember Wendy and all the free spirited cowboys whose ashes are scattered in this one spot near Tonopah. Every year on Memorial Day Bill O'Brien, wearing his boots, his white cowboy hat and a red handkerchief around his neck, accompanied by friends and family, walks across the land of the Eagletail Mountains Wilderness Area to the beautiful garden where the ashes are scattered to pay tribute to his daughter.

It is on these same grounds that he honors life. It was one of those scorching afternoons in the Harquahala Valley, the leaves on the trees stood still, animals had found shades to protect from the scorching sun and there were no birds flying. There was just the majestic hawk standing on O'Brien's hand, panting from the heat. Two black eyes snapped back and forth, her wings poised for the flight. She knew that she was about to let free but there was a hesitation since she has not taken a flight for several months.

This beautiful brown raptor with a white breast and a rust-colored tail, was found several months earlier with an injured wing from a gunshot wound and been brought to the Humane Society. Bill O'Brien visited often with his friends in the Humane Society to check on the wounded animals. He asked if it was possible for him to take care of the wounded hawk and his request was granted. For several months he cared for the wounded bird and taught her to jump on his hand and walk on to his fingers.

After a full recovery the day has come for the hawk to fly free. As she perched on Bill's gauntlet she fluttered her wings, lost her balanced and turned to look at Bill. He gently placed her on his extended finger, "Come on, time to soar, you can do it," Bill whispered.

She erected her head, turned clockwise, looked at the mountains and the gleaming sun, she crouched in a last grip, paused for a moment, looked at her cage and then Bill extended his arm and threw her into the air and with a sudden burst of wings she soared up and away and never looked back.

Bill smiled with pride as he watched the hawk flying into

the far horizon. It was time for more work to help the living. He got on his water truck, ready to drive deep into the desert, as he did regularly to fill the water tanks he placed out there for the deer, antelope, big horn sheep, mountain lions, rabbits, coyotes, and birds. It was a decades-long commitment and a real sacrifice of time and resources, but Bill O'Brien promised himself that, as long as he was alive, he would be sure the birds, rabbits, coyote, deer, desert rats, and other animals always had fresh water to drink.

Since Harquahala Valley was a scarce-water area, he started drip irrigation farming here, one of the early pioneers in Arizona to do it, having learned about it in a trip to Israel where he spoke at the International Jojoba Conference.

Bill started the International Jojoba Growers Association to develop this plant as a viable replacement for whale oil as a lubricant for jet engines, shampoos, cosmetics, and saddle treatment. Besides Jojoba, he grew exotic crops such as guayle, red squill and nopales. In Harquahala, on his Eagletail Farms, he cultivated and produced watermelons, cucumbers, corn, also growing grapes, grains, alfalfa, cotton, almonds, pistachios, plums as well as many herbs and various trees. Bill also had Harquahala Ranches, a recreational desert subdivision with underground utilities and wide streets. On every major street intersection on his ranch, Bill placed regulation-sized, government grade red stop signs. However, instead of the word, "STOP," the signs all read, "WHOA!"

The flight to freedom.

BILL O'BRIEN, NATURALIST

He was tall, lean and handsome. He galloped to Arizona from out of the west with a simple massage: It is your land – Keep it clean! His name, Johnny Horizon. His mission, work together and clean up your towns. Folk singers and Hollywood stars traveled along to help with his mission. They toured the country and gave free concerts, spreading his radical message that the people should take care of their land. It was the late sixties and the environmental movement was sweeping the nation. To recycle trash, preserve water and keep air pollution in check had become major concerns and now to keep America clean and energy efficient had become a national pride.

Johnny Horizon, a fictional character, became bigger than anyone had ever imagined. Two years after his appearance, the first Earth Day event was established in April 1970. Within a few years' time, the countryside clean-ups had spread around the country and now Johnny was asking Americans to do more. He wanted to plant trees to beautify the country. He asked people to be careful with fire, to obey the fish and game laws. Being environmentally friendly has since become a lifestyle. It was no longer a chore but a responsibility.

After the Johnny Horizon Day in 1969, conservation leaders in Arizona were hoping that the public will continue to make every day a cleanup day. Many citizens answered to the call, among them was Bill O'Brien, not out of a sense of duty or obligation, but because it was just the way he was raised, so it was natural. Most of the environmental things he did happened in the day-to-day course of running his ranches and farms.

Near the city of Salome in the Harquahala there was an acre that had become a real public eyesore. It was where the local residents dumped broken cars, tires, old sofas, mattresses, damaged refrigerators and more. Even though it was public land, Bill decided to use his own tractors and he dug a long and deep ditch. He then dumped decades of tons of garbage into the ditch and simply covered it up and left. He just did it because the Earth had been good to him and he wanted to keep it clean. Bill's original goal was just to get rid of the eyesore, but when the ugliness was covered and the excess dirt was smoothed out in its place, there was a long strip of smooth-textured dirt. Bill then got the idea of using that smoothed out strip of land to just make it longer so small air planes could land there. The end result was a functioning airstrip that resembled a small airport with two long driveways to land small planes.

Shortly after the cleanup of the garbage dump and before the ditch was covered with dirt, two people wearing suits approached Bill's doorsteps.

"We are from the Bureau of Land Management," said the first man who was holding a folder. "Are you responsible for the ditch?"

Government men usually were stiff with stern faces and it was difficult to read their emotions, Bill thought that he was in trouble for digging the massive ditch and that he was about to be asked to pay a big fine for digging on public land. In his mind he was preparing his defense, and he sought comfort in the fabled words of George Washington's "I cannot tell a lie. I cut down that cherry tree."

But before Bill could open his mouth the first man jubilantly extended his hand, and gave a hearty, "Congratulations," presented Bill the 1969 Johnny Horizon Award District Award Certificate for cleaning up the environment.

"Thank you, I feel very proud to help clean up the environment," Bill responded.

But what he was feeling was surprise and relief that they said nothing about the airstrip!

While most use the word, environmentalist for people who care about the earth as much as Bill O'Brien, he always called himself a naturalist. It had less of a political connotation. He loved the outdoors; hiking, mountain climbing, riding, camping. He wanted to do it all and he wanted to give to the land.

"Give nature nothing but a good heart, leave nothing but your footprints and enjoy." He would often say.

Besides cleaning up the desert and building an airport out of dirt, he created the Ben Avery wilderness trail and the Eagletail Wildlife Refuge among other numerous environmental undertakings.

He held weekly steak and barbeque events for his employees, for visitors, and for prospective land owners of Harquahala Ranches. He discovered a forty-year old abandoned golf course buried under the desert brush in the middle of Harquahala Valley, had it cleaned up, and organized the First Annual Harquahala Valley Desert Golf Tournament. Instead of golf carts, the players road on horseback. Bill also held polo and lacrosse games on his ranch and he sponsored weekend cattle roping competitions for his Harquahala neighbors and friends.

Everyday there was something going on in Eagletail Ranch at Harquahala Valley.

One of Bill's biggest battles was with Arizona Public Service, not because they were doing bad things, but because they were just so casual and indifferent about where they planned to build their high-tension power lines. Their plan called for these power-lines to go directly through Harquahala Valley, and across farmers' lands, including his, scarring their way through private property in an endless quest for power. After a series of discussions about the details of the proposed path, not about how to best design the path to minimize hardship for residences, Arizona Public Service management and Arizona Planning Commission set a date to meet behind closed doors to make their final decision.

Bill O'Brien had many friends in high places and even more friends in the fields and in the front offices. They knew about the upcoming meeting and they kept their ears to the ground, so to speak, listening and waiting to find out the date, time, and location. The moment had arrived, and Bill got the word. He barreled over to downtown Phoenix to the location of the power-line meeting and went to the door.

"Funny," he thought to himself," I thought closed door meant locked door, but this door is unlocked."

Bill thought back to his University of Arizona history and philosophy classes. He was a big fan of Lord Acton, known as the historian of freedom and the he magistrate of history.

Lord Acton was the one who said "Political atheism: End justifies the means. This is still the most widespread of all the opinions hostile to liberty."

And his most famous expression, "Power tends to corrupt and absolute power corrupts absolutely."

Bill knew what to do. He entered the room, grabbed a chair, dragged it across the polished marble floor making sure it made as much noise as possible .

He pulled the chair right up to the table, and sat down. The surprised looks of eight bureaucrats, technocrats, and engineers, all surrounded by plans and papers and maps, was worth the trip.

"What are you doing here Bill? This is a closed-door meeting," one of them said, who apparently knew Bill by sight.

Bill pushed up the rim of his white cowboy hat, the universal signal of approachability, friendliness and harmlessness.

He approached the table and said with a steady, slow voice, reading the participants' names off their table tent name signs, "Yes, Charlie, you're right, this is a closed-door meeting. And, as you can see, the door is securely closed."

That last crack lightened the mood a bit, so Bill went in head first.

"The route you propose for the high-tension power lines involves the livelihoods of many Harquahala Valley ranchers and their families, including my own," Bill began. "I can tell you this, none of the ranchers likes your plan. They think it's ill-conceived and heavy handed, and it shows insensitivity to Arizona tax-paying citizens. It's understandable why you made this a closed door meeting. But it's just not right."

"As you know Bill, we tried to consider all available routes. This is the best plan possible. There is no other way," another man responded.

That was his cue. Bill smiled, and brusquely pushed away some of their papers that were cluttering the large table. He opened the long, rolled paper he brought along. "Gentlemen, this is the best plan. One that is ecologically, economically, and logically more solid. This plan calls for redrawing the power lines along the more sensible route you see here, thus saving hardship and environmental troubles for the farmers. The only way I was able to devise this alternative route is because I have spent thousands of hours out there, on foot, on horseback, and in the air. There is a better way, it's just that you have to see it from the air in a small aircraft."

There was silence in the room for a moment. "Well, here, take a look and let me explain." Bill broke the silence and unrolled his drawings. After a lengthy explanation the eight people who were going to make the final decision were won over. His plan even saved Arizona Public Service a few hundred thousand dollars because the terrain was easier to prepare for the high tension wires. At the end of the meeting, they all agreed that Bill O'Brien's plan indeed was more logical and ecological, and they agreed, on one condition. They made Bill promise not to mention his little visit to their closed door meeting, or his influence over their decisions. They didn't want more door-busters interfering with their plans.

The high tension power lines were redrawn according to Bill's alternative route. And Bill kept his promise and told nobody about his presence there that day. The Harquahala Valley farmers and residents chalked it up to pure luck that their beautiful land was spared this horrific scar.

Life at the ranch.

THE EAGLETAILS
By *Bill O'Brien*

In the wide, empty spaces of the desert west of Phoenix
there is a great eagle of stone silhouetted against the
sky on an enormous sculpture of red rock called the
Eagletail Mountain

Ol' stone eagle in the sky,
Not preenin' hisself; not gonna fly,
Jes' perched there with his wings half-furled,
Agazin' down on his desert world.

Take a look at him; there he sits,
Like the bird on a U.S.A. two bits.
How long have you been there, Eagle, hey?
Three hundred million years, they say.

I've seen the shark swim over me,
When Arizona was a sea,
Felt pale, soft things grope down my face,
To find their last long resting place,
In that black, cold silent deep,
That lies beneath my feet.
And I have felt the earthquake's blow
But that was a long, long time ago.

I remember the Forty-niners,
Prospectors and hard-rock miners.
Trail-weary, dirty, faces sun-furrowed
All of their grubstake packed on a burro.
Armed with a rifle, a pick, and a shovel,
To tear at my vitals and sift through the rubble,
But I guarded my gold; they found its bright shine,
Off there to the north, at the Vulture Mine.
So the prospectors left me and went on their way,
To the big strikes in Cal-I-for-ni-ay.

The cavalry, bloodied in frontier battles,
Moved America west on McClelland saddles,
Played their deadly hide-and-seek,
With Indians underneath my peak.
Chased down the last Apache band,
To still the way-cry in this land.

Columns of troopers, riding hard,
They opened the trails that chiefs had barred.
Guarded my passes steep and narrow,
Broke at last the India arrow.

What's the one thing above all else,
If you could --- would you grant yourself?
That million-year-old wish would be,
For once --- just once --- to face the West,
See the Great Painter at his best.
Then turn again and once more face,
The East in my accustomed place.

William Howard O'Brien

Sonoran Antelope and Golden Eagle Society.

CHARLIE RUSSELL, LOVER
AND HOME WRECKER

Bill O'Brien's greatest source of his pride and joy and pain and suffering, mixed generously with a lot of Holy Cows! was Charlie Russell, his Texas Longhorn stud bull. Bill loved everything about that irascible bull, perhaps because he reminded Bill so much of himself growing up. Charlie Russell, named after the famous Western artist and storyteller from Montana, did what he wanted, when he wanted, where he wanted, and with whomever he wanted. When Charlie Russell would see a cow flirting at him he would just bellow and jump over or through reinforced cattle corrals, deftly lifting his bull-hood over the barbed wire. He usually destroyed the fence in the process.

According to field reports from the cowboys on the ranch, Charlie was an extraordinary lover, extremely popular with his harem of cows who followed him everywhere. Bill and Charlie Russell had something of a love-hate relationship. You couldn't call it a relationship, really, because it was mostly Bill's problem. Charlie Russell couldn't care less what Bill, or the hard-charging cowboys, or what anyone thought. He was the master and commander of Harquahala Valley. One example of Charlie's temperament was the time Charlie Russell had come to blows with a bull right outside Bill and Sada's ranch house sliding door on their ranch in Harquahala Valley. That day, Charlie decided to crash through the Clanton Corral gate and go for a stroll to enjoy the fresh earthy smells of the moist morning dew. He walked over to start grazing at Bill and Sada's desert oasis in front of their four bedroom ranch home. Bill was out on horseback about two miles away from his ranch home looking for Charlie, the repeat escapee, and the cowboys were out at the Clanton Corral branding cattle. The bull decided to take a swim and went splashing in the deep pond, scattering the catfish and black mollies who feared for their lives, then he lunged out of the pond. As he shook off the excess water, the aggressive bull spied something huge in the ranch house. It was another Texas Longhorn Bull, it was looking right at Charlie. In fact it looked just like Charlie! He had the same cold-steel look in his eyes, the identical six-foot wide longhorns and the same coloring.

Charlie became enraged. If we could read his fearsome mind, he must have been thinking to himself, "There can be only one bull like me in this here outfit."

He lowered his massive head, pawed the earth, snorted once, then raised his head and bellowed so loudly that Bill and his cowboys heard him two miles away.

Charlie Russell then charged full speed at this intruder and crashed into the bull with all his might. The next thing the Texas Longhorn Bull heard were the sounds of shattering glass and metal, tearing and rending of fabric curtains, and the grating, splintering cacophony of overturned wooden tables, bookshelves and chairs. Charlie Russell had charged his own reflection in the sliding glass door of Bill and Sada's ranch house! After stomping around inside the house, bellowing frenetically and pawing some of the Mexican kitchen tiles into powder, he came out the way he went in.

Bill had heard the noise and he galloped his quarter horse,

Sunup, across the two miles of rough, broken desert terrain in a few minutes.

Not knowing what to expect, but prepared for the worst, Bill pulled up the reins of Sunup, vaulted off from the saddle, landed on both feet, and hit the ground running.

Running flat out up to the house, Bill came to a dead stop. He stared at Charlie Russell and couldn't believe his eyes. Then Bill just sat down and started laughing so hard his stomach hurt.

There, in front of the ranch house stood Charles Russell. He was standing triumphantly, with an undefeated attitude His head and longhorns were raised up victoriously, and his back arched to show his full length.

Apparently, Charlie Russell, was oblivious to the fact that he was wearing on his horns the entire ranch house red suede window curtain and parts of a blackout curtain. To top it off, on the left tip of Charlie Russell's horn was the stabbed tattered remains of Sada's white straw floral Easter bonnet.

Still laughing and holding his sides, Bill knew he had to secure that bull before it conquered the entire Valley of the Sun. Bill stumbled over to Sunup to grab his trusty ranch rope. Sure, there'd be heck to pay when Sada found out, but that picture of Charlie Russell was just too funny to stay mad for very long.

Another time Bill and his cowboys were rounding up Charlie Russell and the herd of several thousands, putting them in Clanton Corral, to be loaded onto trucks. Charlie Russell could not stand to be fenced in, so he just jumped over the wooden corral fence, smashing it to pieces, and strutted out into the desert. When Charlie Russell got mad, and he frequently did, he would start charging after the cowboys. As he attacked, he would spray and splatter his bull urine left and right, back and forth, all over him, and all over you if you were close enough. This is about as clear an example of the origin of the word "pissed off." And Charlie Russell was always pissed off. But his harem loved him, the other steers feared him, and the ranch cowboys just wanted to do their jobs and collect their pay without being mangled by this ornery bull with an artist's name, but with a demon's soul.

Meet Charlie Russell.

INVICTUS
By *William Ernest Henley*

Out of the night that covers me,
Black as the pit from pole to pole,
I thank whatever gods may be
For my unconquerable soul.

In the fell clutch of circumstance
I have not winced nor cried aloud.
Under the bludgeonings of chance
My head is bloody, but unbowed.

Beyond this place of wrath and tears
Looms but the Horror of the shade,
And yet the menace of the years
Finds and shall find me unafraid.

It matters not how strait the gate,
How charged with punishments the scroll,
I am the master of my fate,
I am the captain of my soul.

THE IMPLICATIONS OF AN IRISH
AND SWISS F-1 CROSS

Bill and his son Justin, as a kid, would fly the Cessna Taildragger across his seven-hundred-square-mile ranch. When it was time for the cattle to come in from the range, Bill and Justin would be always looking for Bill's cattle, including Charlie Russell and his harem of cows. It was Bill's practice to let his cattle out into the high desert so they could fend for themselves and get tough, and hopefully, get fat. This practice is now called free range, only Bill had been doing it decades.

Once they spotted a stray cow or a small herd of Bill's cattle, they would fly back over to the cowboys out covering the range, Bill would instruct Justin to write something like "Charlie Russell is with his herd of cattle over on the southwest side of Turtleback Mountain." Justin would then toss the lunch bags out the window to the waving cowboys. This was a good system that served them well until GPS tracking and lightweight civilian walkie talkies came along.

Bill had separated his cattle in three categories, the "F-1 Cross." Bill's description of this category was that good cross-breeding can produce smarter, stronger, healthier cattle. That would mean, for example, the bull would be out in the desert and see a tree on top of a hill, and he would deduce that there might be shade and grass there. So he would collect his harem of cows and head up there.

Bill's category of "F-2 Cross" and "F-3 Cross" however, do not have the good sense to turn around and drink from a pond of water behind them.

Years later, in December, 1981, at Bill and Sada's Paradise Valley home, Justin and his fiancée, Anne, were about to be married in the beautiful lush backyard, next to the pool and with a spectacular view of Camelback Mountain. The family and friends were enjoying each other's company and the string quartet was playing Vivaldi's Four Seasons, La Primavera Concerto, Bill and Justin were in the dining room sharing memories of the many adventures they had over the years. The quartet finished the Concerto and stopped. At that moment, Justin's Best Man, Ted Peterson, ever the gentleman, gave him the signal. It was time.

As Justin started to go, he turned to Bill and gave him a hug and a handshake.

"Jus, did I ever tell you about the magic and mystery of the F-1 Cross?" Bill asked.

"Yes, Bill, you did, many times. Thank you," Justin said, as he made a beeline for the door to his bride to be. He had to hurry.

"So anyway…" Bill continued. It was a fascinating and important story that had to be told. The guests could wait, Bill had thought.

The quartet started to repeat La Primavera, again, hoping nobody would notice. Ted, the Best Man, concluded the quartet had only learned one of Vivaldi's four seasons.

"…So, Jus, you know an F-1 Cross, works for people as it does for animals," he continued, deep in the relentless groove of one of his thousands of stories. "In your case, for example, you're about as F-1 as they come. You're pure Irish from my side, and pure English and a touch of Welch from your mother's side.

That's an F-1 Cross. And you know, like cattle, the offspring of F-1 Crosses are smarter, stronger, better looking, and healthier. Now your bride is pure Swiss and German, so she's also an F-1 Cross. So put all that together, and what do you think that means about your future children, Jus?"

The quartet had finished playing La Primavera, a second time, and they had started it up again, now certain that people were noticing the loop. Ted, the Best Man, let it slide because he knew Justin's Dad must be communicating something awfully important to delay his son's own wedding.

"Umm," said Justin, trying not to look at his watch. "That our kids, whenever they decide to get here, if we ever got married, would be in good shape?"

"Close, Jus." Bill said, as if he had all afternoon to chat with his son. "It means, and you better prepare for this, that your children, whether you have a son or a daughter or both, your children will be smarter, stronger, healthier, and better looking than either parent. I can also tell you also from personal experience, an F-1 Cross is a lot harder to handle. They're not necessarily mean, you understand, they just have lot bigger footprint than most kids. Now, this is not a theory Justy, it's scientific fact. It goes all the way back to Gregor Johann in the mid-1800s…"

The quartet had finished playing La Primavera, a third time and they were compelled to play it again, adjusting the tempo upbeat and hoping nobody would notice. Ted, the Best Man, started wondering if Justin was getting cold feet and that maybe Bill was trying to encourage him. Maybe it's time to just grab Justin by the neck.

"So anyway," Bill was saying, "Brother Mendel, as they call him, was a German-speaking Moravian scientist and Augustinian friar who became famous after he died because he was the founder of the modern science of genetics. Farmers had known for centuries about crossbreeding of animals and plants to develop favor certain desirable traits. But Mendel's pea plant experiments established many of the rules of heredity.

So, I just wanted you to be ready for that, Jus. You're going to have some amazing kids. Just be ready to give them a lot of running room so they can fly."

Justin hugged his Dad, said he's absolutely right, and ran out the door to his semi-patiently waiting Swiss bride. The quartet had finished playing La Primavera, a fourth time and, hearing no clue, they were compelled to play it a fifth time, this time adjusting the tempo to a downbeat so it sounded like a funeral march. Ted, the Best Man, ever the gentleman, inadvertently started eating the wedding program.

The Irish and Swiss F-1 cross.

BEAUTY CONTEST IN THE PALM GROVE

"Did you know that I read an article about a beauty contest? I believe it was for the Miss Harquahala Beauty Contest." I asked Bill in one of our last meetings.

"Oh, yes, that was a lot of fun." A smile brightened his face, remembering the amusing past.

"You know, the winner of that contest is a good friend of mine." I told him.

"Really. My golly that was over forty years ago!" he exclaimed.

Beauty contests were popular in the sixties and became a form of entertainment to many American for the next few decades until years later, when the attitude about women competing for beauty lost its appeal. To promote his recreational desert subdivision, in 1973, Bill O'Brien decided to hold a Beauty contest at his recreational desert subdivision, Harquahala Ranches, to attract attention to this beautiful desert acreage. It was really a blend of Beauty Contests, Grape Stomping with huge wine vats, Barbecue and Wine Festival celebration. The venue was at the middle of the palm grove. Bus-loads of contestants, spectators, prospective buyers, the judges, and the media arrived at the palm grove all at the same time. And the stage was the wooden pool decking around a forty-person heated whirlpool, surrounded by tall thick palm trees. The whirlpool was fed by 105° degree water that flowed naturally out of his five-hundred-foot-deep water wells and it was easily the largest man-made naturally heated whirlpool in Arizona.

Bill's perplexed mind was stuck in the history of the beauty contest and he was interested to learn more.

At that moment in The Shedd, Bill looked at me and said, "Sometime ago I heard a story about a contest in Greek mythology. Do you know the story?"

"Yes, Bill," I said, "Beauty contests are not a new revelation – they existed since the beginning of time."

"Of course you know it. I'd like to hear it, if you don't mind."

"The Goddess Eris once threw an apple into the middle of a feast celebrating the wedding of Peleus and Thetis. The apple was to be given to the fairest. Hera, Athena, and Aphrodite all wanted to have it, so the goddesses Eris asked Zeus to judge who was the fairest of them. Reluctant to choose, Zeus decided that Paris, a Trojan mortal would judge them. Each goddess tried to bribe Paris. Hera promised to make him the king of Europe and Asia, while Athena bribed him with wisdom and skill in war. But Paris choose Aphrodite, the goddess of beauty, who offered him the world's most beautiful woman, Helen of Sparta."

Bill took it all in. He asked me how I pronounced "Peleus." He was really wanted to commit what I said to memory. He then continued with his story. He said for this Miss Harquahala competition the beauty contestants will not get an apple but plenty of grapes. They provided the entertainment and an excuse for the small community of grape growers to gather at the date palm oasis for a vineyard celebration. From the first hearty welcome by Grape Ambassador O'Brien, to wine drinking and grape eating, to the last bite of barbecued chicken the contest was a great celebration. The media, guests, and prospective buyers literally ate it up, and they didn't know they could have so much fun out in the desert, away from all the urban stress.

Then Bill said to me, "Remember, Nikos, when you said the goddess Eris asked Zeus to judge who was the fairest of the three, Hera, Athena, and Aphrodite? Well, at the Miss Harquahala Beauty Contest, I actual had Arizona Supreme Court Justices, including my old pal, Justice Charlie Bernstein. After all, if you need a judge, you might as well get a real one." Bill continued with his story. The contestants had to change into swim suits, and dash into the heated giant whirlpool. The Arizona Supreme Court Justices serving as judges sat on deck chairs, judiciously off to the side. Then the contestants would run into the palm grove, change into casual wear, and back again to the poolside for a slow walk and more smiles. The bright Arizona sun shone softly that fine spring day and, the Eagletail Mountains were arrayed in all their glory off in the distant desert. Then the contestants began the stomping of fresh bunches of grapes placed in the vats and the stomping began. After each name was announced, Bill presented her with a basket of grapes. Eventually a winner was announced to be laureled with a grape crown. A fun, frivolous event to be sure. There wasn't very much kissing, hugging, crying or speeches on how to save the world. It was just good clean fun under the smog-free skies. In addition to providing a good time, increased media exposure, and potential sales, Bill's other agenda was to promote Harquahala Valley fruits and produce, and Arizona's wines. He was always thinking about how to promote Arizona's interests and, along the way, some of his own ideas and projects.

At the end of the event, the winner of the Miss Harquahala Beauty Contest was announced.

WIND CATCHER, GRASS
AND
SANDRA DAY O'CONNOR

Environmental concerns was not a new phenomenon. For millennia, human beings have used alternative energy sources in search for conscientious ways to coexist with nature. One of the prime examples is the nineteenth century "Wind Catcher," or "Persian Wind Tower," in the city of Yazd in Iran. Residents of Yazd have since been using wind as an alternative energy source to cool their homes on warm summer days. The Wind Catcher is an ancient Persian architectural element used in various cities in Iran, where the ecological fabric is made up of deserts and the temperature varies greatly between day and night.

The original Wind Catcher includes the combination of a tall tower with several openings at the top to catch the wind from any direction, and an underground canal to store the wind power in addition to being a cooling system. The air caught in the tower openings and then circulated down into the bigger area, creates an airflow. The airflow inside the structure travels in two directions, up and down and creates a cooling effect. As the air is forced downward and into the main area of the building it, is pulled in through a qanat tunnel, which forces air in an upward motion through the tower and exits from one of the tower's opening.

Bill O'Brien was the first known person to design and built of a state of the art environmentally sensitive desert home using the Wind catcher model. Besides the Wind Catcher tower which cooled the inside house air to seventy-eight degrees, he installed a solar power generator and a reflection pond with mosquito-eating black mollie fish. The home was completely off the grid, requiring no power or gas from the utility companies. There were direct flights from Phoenix to O'Brien's airport for interested land buyers. Justin O'Brien was one of the real estate agents for the ranch and he also was the company's private pilot who brought many visitors out to the property.

Bill flew his plane mostly for business, because everything he did was business, even if it was fun. One season, it had rained so much out in the desert that the grass was belly-high. Bill needed working capital so he could buy more cattle and take advantage of the free feed that God had provided. He convinced his business banker to fly out with him in Bill's Cessna to Eagletail Ranches in Harquahala Valley. He flew all over his vast ranch, doing slow lingering turns so the banker could see all the beautiful trees, plants and grass. He wanted his business banker to loan him money so Bill could buy more cattle and run them on the open range of belly high grass. The banker however was not impressed.

"Bill, people that know you, tell me you are one heck of a cowboy and a rancher who cares for his people and his livestock," he said softly.

"But, Bill, my friend," he said looking directly at him, "You've got more grass than credit."

They both smiled at the terseness of that statement. Bill got the loan, anyway, although he can't say if it was from his business banker or from someone else. Even with the extra farmland there was not enough grass in Phoenix to feed his twelve-hundred head of cattle, so he transported the cattle with trucks to Winslow and Flagstaff to be fed. Bill rented a ranch with plenty of grass and transported the cattle with rented trucks, a few hundred every day since each truck will carry thirty-five heads.

Not every flight that left O'Brien's hand-made airport was entertaining. One day Bill took off with his Cessna, carrying his rancher friend Taylor Lawrence and headed to Nogales, Mexico, for the big livestock auction. There was a forecast for a desert dust storm. Bill felt that he could outrun the dust storm but flying over Sanford and approaching Picacho Peak the storm appeared from the east, chasing the small plane and coming fast and furious. The sky darkened as the pilot, desperate to survive the big wind, tried to circle the plane around the dust storm. "Land or go on?" Taylor questioned.

"We could go ahead," Bill said, but after a moment he looked at Taylor and said, "We better land. It is safer. I'm aborting the flight."

He kept circling the plane around the dust storm, climbed steadily, the storm was now stronger and visibility became about zero. Out of a stream of light he saw a patch of land and Bill decided to land there.

As the small plane landed, Bill looked at Taylor with a sigh of relief and said, "That was a close call."

Taylor quickly nodded his head in agreement. After the plane landed a rancher came out to meet them. He introduced himself as Alan Day and helped them secure their plane on the stable and away from the dust storm which by now has become furious. Once inside Bill asked, "Did you say your name is Day? Do you know Sandra Day?

"Yes she is my sister," Alan responded.

"What do you know? This must be the Lazy B Ranch."

Bill answered.

Of course they were talking about Sandra Day O'Connor, the first woman appointed to the U.S. Supreme Court.

"My sister is a busy woman and she does not come to the ranch much."

The three men had a great dinner in the farm and stayed the night. Bill was given the Day's mother's bad to sleep in – it was an honor for sure but is was a bed covered with lace and silk. Bill was thinking "I hope nobody takes a picture with me in this bed,"

They woke up at four in the mornings and after coffee, Bill and Taylor, thanked Alan for his hospitality and took off up to the clear skies, headed for Mexico.

THE HEART OF THE IRISH

Before the idea of a united Irish community in Arizona came into being, there were dozens of independent Irish groups which met separately all year long, but were brought all together only on Saint Patrick's Day. The possibility that a small band of Arizona Irish leaders could unite all these groups to form an Irish Cultural Center seemed impossible until, as luck would have it, Bill O'Brien joined this small group of dreamers. Bill O'Brien is not a big man, even when he is wearing his boots and cowboy hat, he looks small but well put together. But make no mistake, he is a giant in the Arizona Irish community. It all started on a Sunday in the fall of 1996 when Bill O'Brien was invited by his friend, Harry Carroll, a member of the Police Emerald Society, to attend several meetings with various Irish-affiliated groups in the Valley who would be there. Bill's various achievements over the past decades, such as his success with the Wendy Center, an adolescent treatment center that enriched the lives of thousands of troubled young people, had given him a great notoriety both in the press and among various communities.

Harry wanted Bill to see first-hand the complex dynamics of bringing together all the various Irish groups into one united Irish community in Phoenix. Harry, a firebrand and a doer in his own right, knew that it would take someone like Bill O'Brien to unify the many groups, galvanize the Irish in Arizona into action, and power through the incredible obstacles that were preventing the Irish from having their own center of heritage, cultural, and community. After several meetings with the many groups, Bill came to understand why there was no Irish Cultural Center. A plan was forming in his mind.

Bill went into action. He consulted with Howard Adams, who had been elected seven times to the Phoenix City Council. Former Phoenix Mayor Skip Rimsza remembered Howard "as a master deal maker… and the smoothest politician I've ever seen."

Always gracious, Howard was the consummate negotiator. He knew that there was always another deal down the road, and there was no sense making enemies. He had such style. Bill knew that Howard was proud of his Irish roots, and, according to his obituary, he would drive his motorized wheelchair down Central Avenue in St. Patrick's Day parades. He led Phoenix's first delegation to Ennis, Ireland, in 1990, and was instrumental in establishing its sister-city status. Howard was to be one of Bill's behind the scenes mentors to make the Irish Cultural Center a reality. Ken Clark also played a key role with Bill in helping identify and attract more than thirty Irish-affiliated groups to assemble.

Next, Bill printed up some stationery and designed it as The Irish Coalition. He had printed on it the heads of all the dozens of Irish-related organizations in the Valley of the Sun. This included Irish bag piper societies, dancing groups, history clubs, genealogy clubs, Gaelic and Irish language clubs, musical clubs, St. Patrick's Day committees, you name it. He made the stationery look like everyone was already a part of the Irish Coalition. Then he sponsored the largest private dining room at the University Club in downtown Phoenix and invited them all to attend at noon.

At the University Club, all the leaders of the dozens of

Irish clubs had assembled. Everybody who was anybody in the Irish community was there. They were delighted to see authentic Irish Punt coins set out as luncheon favors. Ken Clark was holding everything together for the main event. And Bill O'Brien was late. As they all sat down for lunch, Ken rose to welcome them. Just then, the doors to the University Club dining room flew open, and a very dusty Bill O'Brien barreled into the room. Before proceeding into the dining room, as Bill told it to this author, he either figuratively or actually locked the doors to the exit

"My apologies for being late to my own luncheon," he said briefly, taking off his cowboy hat and whacking it against his dust-covered Levis. "One of my cowboys left the gate open on my ranch and all the cattle got out. The cattle are back in, and the cowboy is grateful he's not on the way out." The Irish leaders chuckled. They'd all been in situations like that, although maybe not as dusty.

"My heartfelt thanks to Ken Clark, Howard Adams, and all of you present for assembling here today." Bill continued, "The purpose of this meeting is that we have got to unite the Irish in Arizona. We need to form our own Irish Cultural Center. For this to work, we can't have any problems with your religion, or your politics, or your centuries of perceived or actual injustice. Now to do this is going to take money, a lot of it. Money from you, from your Irish clubs you head up, from your friends, and family, and from all who want to see an Irish Cultural Center in downtown Phoenix. You'll notice there's no booze in this room and the doors are locked, so we're going to get through this pretty darn quick. Now how're we going to fire this up?"

While Bill's speech was compelling, despite his rustic look, not everyone in these diverse Irish groups knew who Bill O'Brien was.

Someone from the group of leaders yelled out, "Who are you to be our leader and where do you fit in?"

Bill, as usual, had the answer. Pulling down his cowboy hat to just over his eyes, he declared, "I'm the head honcho of the Irish Cowboys Association. Now turning this meeting over to my friend, Ken Clark..." and without blinking an eye, Bill immediately turned the podium over to the well-known and respected in the Irish community Ken Clark who did a great job explaining the goals that could be accomplished by a united Irish community. With the backing of City Councilman Howard Adams, right there behind the locked doors of the University Club, the seed of an Irish coalition in Phoenix was planted and began to germinate.

At that point, attorney Jim Cunningham chimed in with a very generous donation. Sean Lee joined as well. That got the ball rolling. Ken Clark passed to the group a sheet of paper, and everyone contributed very generous amounts of cash, checks and pledges. A non-profit corporation was formed for the group and in the first Founders luncheon at the University Club. Nearly one-hundred-thousand dollars was raised in less than one hour.

After lunch, as Bill recalls it, he collected all the funds and put them into his cowboy hat for safekeeping. He then went down to the Mayor's office, still dusty from his unplanned cattle stampede. The Mayor's secretary, knowing from prior visits that Bill would not leave until the Mayor came out, buzzed her chief, who came out right away.

"Mayor," Bill said, "Apologies for my attire. Cattle stamped out at the ranch. I have here about one-hundred-thousand-dollars in cash, checks, and pledges to build an Irish Cultural Center in downtown Phoenix. Together, with the matching funds promised by the City of Phoenix, Arizona Department of Transportation, other departments, and our more than thirty

Irish-affiliated groups, we are ready to get started today, what do you say?" Bill plunked down all the money on the Mayor's table.

"Great job, Bill," the Mayor said, looking at all the paper and pledges. He thought he even saw Irish Punt coins. "I'll form a committee and we'll get going on this Irish Cultural Center right away. Now maybe you should get back to your cattle before they come looking for you."

Bill O'Brien, Ken Clark and Howard Adams became instant friends. Bill, a rancher with the knowledge on how to organize communities to work together for a common goal, and Ken Howard, knowledgeable in the ways of the City of Phoenix operating mechanism, seemed like the perfect team to unity. After two more meetings at the city hall, a steering committee of Howard Adams, Ken Clark, and Bill O'Brien was elected to keep the Irish enthusiasm of a united Irish community growing.

Bill suggested that the old timers would be recognized and keep on helping the growth of the Phoenix Irish community and his only condition was to leave religion and politics out of the mission statement, but include all Celts without exception. "The Celts are a race that immigrated from somewhere around the Red Sea through the centuries. One-eighth Celtic blood would qualify for Irish, which is the formula used by the federal government to recognize those of American Indian heritage. It is a challenge but no tougher than running a desert cattle ranch for thirty-five years." Bill O'Brien said on a speech in the gathering of the leaders of all twenty-four Irish organizations in Arizona Club in 1998.

Since that day, the Irish Cultural and Learning Foundation never looked back. Maureen O'Mahar, owner-editor of The Desert Shamrock gave outstanding support, which helped unite all the Irish organizations in the Valley of the Sun. Ann

Neimann took over the newspaper to keep the flame of Irish pride alive in Arizona through her wonderful revamping of "The Desert Shamrock."

The City of Phoenix had proposed a small parcel of land closed to the Phoenix Library but the Irish leadership had bigger plans. They decided to go after two- acres on the west side of Central Avenue. It took almost a year for the city's red tape about various factors to go through, but persistence got the job done. Howard Adams and Bill O'Brien felt it would be a fine time to encourage the Irish Monument Committee to raise funds and build the monument on the property. Artist Maureen McGuire designed the Great Hunger Memorial, "An Gorta Mor" taken from the many ancient dolmens seen in Ireland. The impressive monument was constructed before the deal of the land was made and it was a gamble for Howard and Bill since they would have to refund the money for the memorial if the deal of the property didn't work out. Now the monument stands on the property to demonstrate the mutual trust between the Irish community and the City of Phoenix. After the City of Phoenix had made the property at 1106 North Central Avenue available for the Irish Center, the Foundation put together in cash, labor, matching funds and material contributions, a total of over two-million-dollars to finance the Great Meeting Hall and the Irish Cultural Cottage. Due to Phoenix architect Paul Ahern's insistence on authentic Irish design, the Center is a historic landmark, adding culture and charm to downtown Phoenix.

It was O'Brien's influence with city leaders and businessmen that helped bring the Irish community together. Achieving this was altogether impressive since it is known how headstrong the Irish could be.

When Bill was getting support among Arizona Irish to build

the Irish Cultural Center in downtown Phoenix, he took Bishop Thomas O'Brien, the Roman Catholic Bishop of Phoenix out to lunch. Bill knew that many Irish in Arizona were Catholic, and he wanted all the help he could get to get the Irish Center off the ground. Bishop O'Brien, listening to the colorful adventures Bill was telling him, asked what his faith was.

Bill knew that, with a name like O'Brien, if he lived in Ireland he would be Catholic. But, ever since Bill flunked Confirmation, because of that boxing match he had with the other guy on the way to Confirmation over how many Hail Mary's the boys had to say, Bill later in life became Episcopalian. He always made sure son Justin and daughter Wendy went to church on Sunday. Justin later served as an acolyte, and sang in the St. Barnabas Church of the Desert in Paradise Valley. But Bill's many entrepreneurial business ventures kept him out of town most Sundays.

What to tell the Bishop?

Without missing a beat, Bill started to sing to Bishop O'Brien an old 1950s cowboy song by Western singer Red Foley:

"Oh, the place where I worship is the wide open spaces
Filled by the hand of the Lord
Where the trees of the forest are like pipes of an organ
And the breeze plays an amen choir.

All the stars are the candles and they light up the mountains
Mountains are altars of God
Oh, the place where I worship is the wide open spaces
Where the sun warms the peaceful sod."

The Bishop of The Roman Catholic Diocese of Phoenix was impressed, both with Bill's singing and with his authentic, honest, and creative answer. He gave Bill his full support and promised to spread the word about the new Irish Cultural Center.

With children and grandchildren.

LOS SAN PATRICIOS

Bill O'Brien wanted to expend the Irish culture into another culture he loved: The Spanish. Bill was inspired by the story about Los San Patricios, a story he heard decades ago while traveling for his wool business. It wasn't until a beautiful night in the late nineties while sitting outside his ranch, exchanging stories with an El Charro that he was reminded about the history of the Irish and the Mexicans during the Mexican-American war in 1846. Shortly after that night, Bill visited his friend Hector Corona in his Corona Ranch in south Phoenix to ask him for help to create a cross-cultural group.

Hector a first-generation Mexican-American, had heard about Los San Patricios from his parents and was willing to help Bill with his connections in the Mexican community.

Bill O'Brien was able to form an organization called, Los San Patricios of Arizona. There were no formal meetings for this group, just an annual celebration and to participate in St. Patrick's Day parades in downtown Phoenix.

The people of these two cultures are comparable when celebrating, since both love to drink, dance and sing. There are similarities when it comes to family and country; respect of the elder, love for the children, work ethics, pride for their heritage and so much more.

Many of the Irish identified more with the Mexicans not only because they were Catholic but also because of the parallels in the oppression the people of both countries suffered at the hands of powerful countries, especially the Irish who, for almost ten centuries, England attempted to oppress Ireland and the Irish resistance to being subjugated. Religion has historically played a very large role in shaping the conflict. However religious beliefs were not the only motivating element in the conflict, despite the fact that most of the followers to one side are Catholics and on the other side being Protestants.

The principal component for English control over Ireland was motivated by land ownership and it was to be achieved through military adventures and legislative acts. Land, to all empires in the past, was extremely important because it is the origin of economic power, that which makes it possible to increase military power and to engage in political influence. The two ethnic groups share more than that, during the Mexican-American War, a large number of Irish-American soldiers fought with the Mexicans and were dubbed "El Battallon de los San Patricios."

There are monuments and statues in Mexico City honoring the Irish people. Some say the Irish soldiers were prisoners of war and were forced to fight on the Mexican side. Others say the Irish defected willingly because of the promise of a land grant and to flee discrimination in the United States. Bill O'Brien had his own spin.

"If a gringo writes it, it's Those traitors!" he said. "If the Mexicans write it, it's Those heroes!"

"The average Mexican knows this," O'Brien said. "They're taught we're good guys and friends."

Bill O'Brien's title is El Capitan for his Mexican association.

"Our whole purpose is to respect our neighbors and the similarity in character between both groups," O'Brien said.

Los San Patricios de Arizona was formed in 1997 by

O'Brien who had managed to round up nearly one thousand member the first year alone.

The group's participation in the parade includes members of Irish and Mexican descent. The men are dressed as Los Charros wearing traditional Mexican pants and short jackets, spurs and sombreros and the women participate in competitive precision side-saddle. And of course there is Mariachi music, drinking and dancing.

There are no dues, fees or meetings for members just a sharing of common character. "The Mexicans love the Irish, and the Irish love the Mexicans," Bill says. "Both groups have a love of family and fun and have a strong work ethic."

The fact is that in 1845 many Irish left their country during the failure of the potato crop and headed to America. They were offered jobs fighting in the Mexican-American War. Some Irish decided to help the Mexicans and, under the leadership of John Riley, formed the San Patricio Battalion. The Irish fought valiantly in five battles, and although the Mexicans lost, they honored their Irish heroes with medals, plaques and ceremonies.

Each year, in addition to the parade, Los San Patricios de Arizona celebrates the one-hundred and fifty-year bond between the two ethnic groups.

Despite the issues surrounding illegal immigration, O'Brien insists that the group should fly above that fray. "The purpose of Los San Patricios de Arizona is to work to create friendships between Mexico and Arizona," O'Brien said. "It has nothing to do with religion or politics."

Knowing Bill O'Brien is to know that he loves his country, he is as American as they come. There are no motives for his cross-cultural respect other than that he understands that to live in a world that coexists in harmony, to respect and honor those who are worthy of, and that his two other beloved cultures, the

Irish and the Mexicans are to share their common passions. Evidence is his gesture to his friend Felix Corona. Felix Corona, a Mexican immigrant spent the past fifty years working to support his family of nine.

Bill and Felix been friends for several years. Bill, impressed with Felix's work ethics, loyalty and character, had decided to name a mountain on his ranch after Corona and honored his friend in a ceremony in 2005 when Bill unveil the new name. Bill said the mountain he is naming after Corona has been nameless since he bought the property nearly fifty years ago. It is a peak in the Eagletail Mountains, it towers two-thousand feet above the desert floor. It has a four-pointed summit looking like a "corona."

"This guy has done a lot," O'Brien said. "Imagine coming here and not even speaking English. That took courage at that age to do that and now he's very successful. This is a good man and it's time for him to be recognized."

Corona left Jalisco, Mexico in 1947. As an ambitious teenager who did not know English but was desperate for work. Corona took whatever job he could find in the fields, picking and packing fruit in California and Arizona. Bill O'Brien and Felix Corona are heroes within the Hispanic and Irish community. "We always liked those guys anyway," says Bill O'Brien, who learned to speak perfect Spanish. "The Irish and the Mexicans have always liked the same things: family, work, singing and drinking!"

Bill and Felix.

1.

THE LONG JOURNEY

It is September 15, 2015. As I walked to the front door of the O'Brien's home, a place that I have been so many times by now, the routine to follow was a familiar one. I knocked with the bronze door knocker on the old wooden door, the Rhodesian Ridgeback's footsteps click on the tile flooring will stop behind the door. A few moments later the door opened and Rosa, the Spanish young woman, said, "Buenos dias, señor" and welcomed me into the O'Brien's home. Bill will be up from his chair already, walking briskly towards me. Justin rises, but waits for Bill to greet me. His wife, Sada, will be sitting quietly in her chair looking outside the class patio door.

"El Griego," Bill will exclaim, with that illustrious smile of his.

He shook my hand. I walked behind Sada, touched her shoulder, and she smiled and held my hand.

"How are you dear," I asked.

"Better now that you are here," she responded.

We sat around the round table and talked for a few minutes, and then we headed out the back toward The Shedd. My entrance to O'Brien's home was the only routine I was used to, beyond that nothing was predictable. This was possibly the last time to interview Bill O'Brien. It was just the two of us. We approached the back building. It was nearing the end of the hot season, just before noon. The morning rain cleared the air, the grounds were still a bit wet and the temperature was unusually comfortable. The grapevines were in full bloom, climbing the walls of the building, and several fig trees near the side wall. "Grapes and figs," I commented.

"Do you like them?" Bill asked.

"Of course, I love figs and grapes, I am Greek!"

"Let me see if they are ready to eat." Bill walked to a fig tree, pulled down a fig, took a bite and then spit it out, "Not ready yet," he said with a disapointing tone in his voice.

We stopped in front of the door, he looked at me and said, "Let's not go into The Shedd today. Let's sit in the back."

In the back there were a few chairs sourounded by trees. We sat overlooking the Camelback Mountain and he began to tell a story, but I gently interupted him. "Let's talk about whatever comes to mind today. No stories, just talk," I said.

His face brightened with excitment, and he said, "I like that, let's do it. It would be like we just met."

Then he pulls out one of his cowboy business cards from his shirt pocket, hands it to me and says, "Nice to meet you!" "When I had the ranch this is the business card I gave when I met someone."

The card had just his name, phone number, and Sun Up brand. "I said, If you see a cow with that brand on it, please call me, because that's my cow."

I smiled thinking that Bill at ninety-two years old he still carries a young spirit.

"What is one of the most vivid memories still intact in your mind?" I asked.

"The Elephant, that beautiful creature. I could not pull the trigger."

"Really!"

"Yes, that majestic animal had a great effect on me."

"I know you admired your father. What was one of the best advices he gave you?"

"He always told me to stay out of fights. One thing for sure though, don't even fight a lawyer or a newspaper, because they can fight back wholesale."

"What about the most unusual thing?"

His mind seemed to travel back in to the long past. "There are so many," he murmured, "Here, I got one. It was in the Parada del Sol, I don't remember the year. I had a couple of drinks and I was hungry, we were going by the Safari Hotel in Scottsdale, so I left the parade and rode my horse right in to the dining room. Then I walked the horse around a couple of tables. Then I tipped my hat and walked out."

Okay, now I am speechless – what could you say about that!

"Talking about mistakes, have you ever forgiven someone who wronged you?"

He did not have to think about this one. "Forgiveness is part of your personal inner peace. It is not always easy to forgive. Every time I forgave someone I felt brave. Like that time I caught a cattle rustler in my ranch and had him put in jail in Florence prison, then I visited him just before he got out, bringing cigarettes and candy. Why did you do it, Jim? Why did you rustle my cattle? You're a terrific cowboy, you didn't need to do it."

"What did he say? Was he sorry for what he did?" I asked.

"Not really. He told me, Bill, it's just so much darn fun! I forgave him anyway."

I struggled for questions for a man who seemed like he had accomplished everything he wanted to in life. From the young entrepreneur to a Golden Glove Boxing Champion, Polo Player, Scuba Diver, Private Pilot, Bronc Rider, Wild Horse Tamer,

Roper, Archer, Horse jockey, Sailor, Yachtsman, Alligator roper, Tennis, Golf, Dog breeder, Frogman, Pigeon raising. He was a Practical Joker, Conservationist, Storyteller, Poet, Community Activist, and the list goes on.

"What was the craziest thing you did to impress a girl?"

"Well, I roped an alligator in Louisiana!" he smiled as he noticed the surprised expression on my face. "I knew she was watching and I was good at roping, so I wanted to show off. I roped the alligator but he was so strong. If I did not let the rope go he would have pulled me in the water. If not that, the beast could have started roiling up the rope, you know, they spin round and round, and he could have roiled right up my horse's rear end and made a meal out of me. All I got from the girl for my trouble was a laugh and a smile. Seems like a fair deal."

"Whom do you consider a good friend?"

"Besides you?" he said with a straight, honest face. "Someone that takes time out of a busy schedule to visit a friend in the hospital, especially if the old friend is down and nearly out." A pleasant sun was tilting west of the mountain, creating a nice shade in the back yard. My mind traveled in the past, to some of the things I have heard or read about him. For almost twenty years, Bill wrote over five-hundred newspaper columns for the Central Arizona newspapers in Gila Bend, Buckeye, and Casa Grande. Frequently compared to Will Rogers for their short, pithy commentary, written in the conversational language of the cowboy. Bill's "Ol' Bill Says," always had three qualities: His topics were as true today as the day they were written. They always revealed something of Bill's character. They always had a zinger of an ending to make you think.

Here's a sample from his columns.

FOR THE FARMERS: "I see back in Washington they've taken the food out of the agriculture department and shipped it over to the Secretary of State. Getting so a feller don't know who's working for what world anymore. But they sure ought to keep a strong spokesmen in Washington who represents just the farmers. One feller says it's all for "Detente" but another feller who's running for President of the United States said the other day he didn't understand exactly what "Detente" meant. Well, I don't either. The way the rest of the world is laughing at us, I thought it could be a Brooklyn description of the situation "day taunt."

ON ILLEGAL WORKERS: "Well, they are picking up the 'illegal aliens' again and also the people who hire them. I notice they have cleaned up the name to 'undocumented aliens.' These men sleep under the orange trees during the harvest for several reasons: it's cheaper, the unions can't recruit at night in private orchards, and in Arizona, sleeping under October skies is a pleasure. Maybe they ought to change the name to 'Foreign Exchange Students' and give college credit in orchard management."

ON FREE ENTERPRISE: "Damocles was a blacksmith in the old days and he invented the double-edged sword. The soldiers had trouble at first on the battlefield with the 'Sword of Damocles' because, on the back-swing, they sometimes cut down their own people. Well, the free enterprise system generally works about the same way. A double-edged sword means, you give and you get!"

ON FIGHTING INFLATION: "I see where the President's Council on Wage and Price stability is going to use economic pressure to fight inflation. The government says they are now going to help hold prices down, particularly food, by switching purchases to other items if prices rise too high. Well, I am sure happy, as a taxpayer, that they figured out this new system. Most mothers started using the same system years ago...it's called 'shopping.'"

ON SPIN DOCTORS: The Washington 'spin doctors' have come up with a new word for the politicians. It is a fact that the more confused the American voters are, the easier they are to lead. So, the newest word back there is, SINPIE, the letters spell out the meaning: Substance Is Nothing, Perception Is Everything! Hopefully, with the lightning communication we have today, America just won't buy this malarkey anymore."

Someone from the house brought ice tea, fruits and nuts, interrupting Bill's story and my thoughts. It was a good opportunity for questions. "Bill, you have done so much. What is it that you recollect the most – from all that you accomplished?"

He looked at me, and I could see there was a momentary thought process. Then he said, "Let me ask you the same question, since you have lived a full life as well!"

I wasn't surprised. Bill is a conversationalist, he is a storyteller. On second thought, Bill O'Brien was not really a storyteller. He was just telling stories in a compelling manner about his extraordinary life. This Question-and-Answer format was not his style. I was not sure if he realized it or not but he was using the Socratic method of questioning, – Answer with a question.

"What do you want to know?" I responded.

"I am interested in how you have grown in such self-control. I never heard you talk bad about anyone, you are always respectful and positive. What are your beliefs?"

"Bill, my friend, you and I have made a promise – not to talk about religion and politics."

"Yes, I know, although we both agreed that religion and God was needed in our life but we have a difference of opinion as to why. And politics in Washington...well, at least it's entertaining. But tell me what you really are all about?"

"The short answer is that I believe in logic, I trust science."
I told Bill. "Things have to make sense for me in order to
comprehend them."

"Give me an example how it works."

"Well, throughout the years I struggled to identify the
virtues upon which to base my personal growth. After much
searching I decided to work on gaining Wisdom, to live my life
with Courage, to define Justice and focus on Temperance."

Bill got up, walked around, in deep thoughts, his hands
behind his back, circled around a tree, then stood next to me,
examined my head and said, "I always wondered what was under
that thick hair of yours. By-the-way you have a nice haircut. I
think I will let my hair grow long and get a haircut like yours!"

"What!"

He sat back down and I waited for him to talk.

"Okay, back to our subject. You believe in these virtues.
That makes a lot of sense. I believe in the same things but
what about Faith, Honor, Love?"

"Of course, all are important. Simply, I wanted to be defined
by the virtues I have chosen to grow with. I believe what defines
you, Bill, are principles. You are the epitome of principles."

"Why principles, aren't they the same as virtues?"

"Not exactly Bill. It is a bit complicated."

"I tried to be a good man, to be fair and faithful, to have
respect and honor, but I also wanted to succeed in everything I
do." Bill stated.

"And you did. It is what makes you an extraordinary human
being. However you just gave yourself the answer about virtues
and principals."

"Explain how I did that" Bill said.

"Unfortunately, my friend, you cannot have it all. Perfection
does not exist, it is an illusion. You come pretty close, though."

"So, let me understand what you are saying. We are both seeking goodness but going on a different path to get there," Bill said.

"Pretty much, for me to accomplish my individual growth I have to prioritize my virtues and accept what others call 'failures.' A 'failure' for me is a lesson, not a tragedy. The only failure in life would be to betray my virtues. Everything else, like wealth, fame and the likes are alternate concerns. Principles on the other hand, do not allow you to 'fail.' Even though you are guided by the same moral compass, you are concerned with the consciousness of failure. We are both seeking morality, but through different avenues. One thing that bonds our ideologies is values."

"Interesting, I have to think about all this tonight. It is getting late. Are you hungry?"

"I could eat something."

The sun was tilting to the western horizon, a few white clouds were hanging above the mountaintop.

"Come on Griego, let's go up to the Elements restaurant for dinner at the Sanctuary on Camelback Mountain." he said. "I hear the food is great, and the view is spectacular." We walked back to the house. Bill had an amazingly steady walk for his age. He was quiet, deep in thought. We opened the back door.

Sada was watching television, "You were out there for a while," she said.

"Sada, I love you. We are going to diner. Do you want to come?"

"No, I am okay. But you have to rest first"

"Sada, I can't rest now, I am too excited!"

We were back up at the Elements Restaurant at the Sanctuary Resort, where we met for the first time. For most of us the quest, like Odysseus, to find our Ithaca, is an endless journey. But for Bill O'Brien, there was no question that he has found his. It is up here, on this Camelback Mountain, in the realm of nature's harmony, where he embraces life. While he was looking at the valley under the illuminating sun, I pause for a moment to marvel his serene expression. It is in such environment where the insanity of wars, the bickering of politics, fear, doubt, the struggle for everyday survival, it is a place where for a moment or two nothing matters, death, wealth, hate, envy, all surrender to the nature's sorcerous beauty. I imagined all his memories compiled under the shadows of his beloved Camelback Mountain; where he spent most of his life, where his children played, where he and Sada found their Nirvana. A few clouds had appeared in the sky, just ahead of the now meager sun.

"You and I met right here for the first time," he said, with a melancholic tone on his voice.

This is a different side of Bill O'Brien than the one I have interacted with for the past year. The witty, smiling, bigger-than-life persona, the center of attention without meaning to be, suddenly hidden behind melancholic thoughts.

"I've had a good life," Bill O'Brien said looking across the twinkling Paradise Valley below. "I've seen this unincorporated area of Maricopa County grow into the well-run Town of Paradise Valley. Heck, I was part of the committee that founded it." The sun was descending in the far west, touching the clouds, its day's work was about done.

He turned to me and said, "Once you said that you have no regrets about life, that you may not have as much as many others, but you have more than most. I like that," he shook his head for a moment, "Yes, I like that!"

I don't remember, really, when I said that but I was surprised that he did.

I simply said, "No regrets, my friend."

He looked at me with those blue eyes and smiled, a smile

that lightened his entire being. "You know, Nikos," he said, "When I tell people some of my theories and they have doubts about what I say, about the truthfulness of it, I clue them in so they're not sore at me. I tell them; If it ain't true, it ought to be!"

Here is the Bill I know, welcome back!

"Well, Bill, I believe that you also tell people that you always want to reinvent the wheel because the original one has too many corners."

He laughed out loud, "I do, yes, that's funny. I don't know how I come up with those things. They just pop up in my head and I just have to say it."

"What was one of the best things you have done in your life?"

"Moving to Arizona."

"Really! After all you have done?"

"I love it here."

"Who's one of your best friends?"

"Sunup, my horse Sunup. I miss him."

"What makes you proud?"

"My son, Justin."

"What else do you miss?"

"Wendy, our daughter who is no longer with us. I miss her every day."

"What about your biggest disappointment?"

A smile, "Are you trying to trick me? No regrets – remember?"

I smile.

"And your biggest love?"

"Sada, the love of my life. Nothing else comes close."

The clouds had moved closer, a gentle rain began to fall, refreshing the thirsty desert earth. It was time to go. We walked outside.

"I love the smell of the earth after the rainfall," I said.

"Water is life," Bill responded.

"I've said that," I told him.

"What? Now we argue who said what!"

We looked at each-other and laughed.

"Come on buddy. I have to take you home."

Life – Bill O'Brien he had definitely defined the meaning of living a full life.

It has been a long journey for Bill O'Brien, but it always seemed like his journey was just beginning every time the sun rose in the eastern skies.

The Last Dance.

AUTHOR'S BIO

Award winning author, Nikos Ligidakis, born and raised in Greece, came to America in 1969, at the age of twenty-four.

While in America, he began to write with clarity and passion in an ardent voice, not to just recount adventures, but with expressions of feelings, to encourage the reader to think, to find hope in the eternal struggle for the meaning of life and the perception of harmony.

In his extremely popular book, *"The Heroes of my Thoughts,"* Ligidakis has written a warm and loving tribute to his lifelong heroes, his parents. The book became the genesis for the "Children's Pen Foundation" a non-profit educational program founded by Nikos in 2001 to inspire 6th and 7th graders to develop writing skills by composing short stories and poetry with the common theme "What kind of hero does our world need today?"

In his award-winning book, *"The Last Mission,"* Ligidakis introduced us to a hero in a fascinating story of survival during World War II. This incredible story narrates this hero's freedom run of hundreds of miles in enemy territory full of danger, exhaustion, starvation, and death.

His book he calls "The work of my lifetime," *"Power and Defiance,"* is a labor of love, a nearly 800-page book about the integrity of individual freedom and the intense struggle for social justice. Such deep matters require not only the profound thoughts in the writing, but also equal reflective thoughts in the reading. The reader will find such thoughts throughout the pages of *"Power and Defiance,"* and hopefully will be challenged to recognize the heroism of those individuals who are perceived to be ordinary and simultaneously re-examine the character of those who proclaim themselves to be righteous and just.

Today Nikos devotes his life to coaching new authors, encouraging and assisting them to write and publish their books. His publishing company, Inkwell Productions, has attracted numerous new and published authors and it's rapidly becoming a significantly growing influence in changing the traditional face of publishing.

Nikos has founded several charitable organizations with the most notable his Thanksgiving Project to Feed the Hungry, a program that provided food to hundreds of thousands during its 21-year run. His selfless work with people has earned him several humanitarian awards over the years.

Ligidakis lives in Scottsdale, Arizona and has three children and six grandchildren.

Nikos Ligidakis

.

www.ingramcontent.com/pod-product-compliance
Lightning Source LLC
Chambersburg PA
CBHW030531100426
42813CB00001B/215